A Struggle Against Great Odds

Albert Dittes

TEACH Services, Inc.
PUBLISHING
www.TEACHServices.com • (800) 367-1844

All rights reserved. No part of this publication may be reproduced, distributed, or transmitted in any form or by any means, including photocopying, recording, or other electronic or mechanical methods, without the prior written permission of the publisher, except in the case of brief quotations embodied in critical reviews and certain other noncommercial uses permitted by copyright law. For permission requests, write to the publisher, TEACH Services, Inc., at the address below.

Copyright © 2022 Albert Dittes
Copyright © 2022 TEACH Services
ISBN-13: 978-1-4796-1146-1 (Paperback)
ISBN-13: 978-1-4796-1147-8 (ePub)
Library of Congress Control Number: 2021935406

The website references in this book have been shortened using a URL shortener and redirect service called 1ref.us, which TEACH Services manages. If you find that a reference no longer works, please contact us and let us know which one is not working so that we can correct it. Any personal website addresses that the author included are managed by the author. TEACH Services is not responsible for the accuracy or permanency of any links.

Published by

www.TEACHServices.com • (800) 367-1844

Table of Contents

1. Introduction	**7**
2. The Southern Backdrop	**10**
3. The Conference Founders	**17**
• A Quick Overview	17
• Starting Out	18
• Back to Tennessee	19
• His Work Bore Fruit	20
• Starting More Churches	21
• Splitting One Conference into Two	22
• Highs and Lows in Kentucky	22
• Duty Calls Him Back to Struggling Tennessee	23
• Problem of Underserving the Members	24
• Back to Concentrating on Kentucky	24
• Hard Work Paying Off	25
• Help from the North Finally on the Way	26
• Mob Violence	26
4. Other Early Workers	**30**
• G.K. Owen	32
• Patrick D. Moyers	35
• Samuel Fulton	36
• Charles M. Kinney	39
• William Covert	41
5. Early Prominent Families	**46**
• The Dortch Family	46
• The Lowry Family	49
• The Yates Family	50
• Other Early Families of Significance	53
6. The Law Challenges the Sabbath	**54**
• Pressure on West Tennessee Believers	54
• Valuable Advertising	55
• Wider Impact	56
• More Trouble in West Tennessee	57
• Attention Shifts Eastward	68

- Harassment Backfires ... 72
- Positive Results ... 76
- An Era Starts to Close ... 77

7. Later Important Workers ... **80**
- E.E. Marvin ... 80
- H.W. Reed ... 82
- Charles L. Boyd ... 85

8. Kentucky Develops ... **90**
- Limited Resources Blunt Impact ... 91
- Positive Spin on Struggles ... 92
- Reorganization ... 92
- More Evangelism ... 93
- Money a Constant Problem ... 93
- New Leadership ... 94
- Outside Help ... 94
- Still Possibilities ... 95
- Financial Problems Still Hurt ... 95
- Evangelism Continues ... 96
- Still Can't Lick the Financial Problem ... 97
- New Leadership ... 97
- A Low Point ... 98
- Powerhouse Minister Starts His Career ... 98
- Work in Small Places Continues ... 99
- Some Response in Eastern Kentucky ... 100
- Victory in Louisville ... 100
- Another Setback ... 101
- A Strategy for the Larger Cities ... 102
- Nothing Stops Evangelism ... 102
- Some Sacrifice Comforts of Home ... 104
- Looking Up ... 104
- A Miracle Saves the Day ... 105
- Penetrating Unentered Areas ... 106
- A Lasting Impact ... 106
- Results ... 107

9. East Tennessee Develops ... **108**
- Early Carolina Connections ... 108
- More People Respond in Other Areas ... 109

- More Opposition — 109
- Threats Fail to Intimidate — 110
- Inroads in Other Places — 110
- Effective Evangelism Among the Blacks — 112
- The Message Spreads Still More — 112
- Sabbath Work and Over-Extension Problems — 114
- Promoting the School — 115
- Progress Continues — 116
- Persecution Won't Go Away — 116
- The Charges Enlarged Their Audience — 117

10. Epilogue — **118**

Introduction

Adventism started slowly in Kentucky and Tennessee. Growing new believers to maturity in these states was hard during the post Civil War years. Churches to give new converts encouragement and support simply did not exist, not to mention conferences to pay ministers. The great pioneers like James and Ellen White, Joseph Bates, J.N. Loughborough, Hiram Edson, John Nevins Andrews and others had left a big mark in the North.

Humanly speaking, introducing Adventism to Kentucky and Tennessee would seem impossible during this juncture of history because people there just weren't too responsive to anything coming out of a northern city like Battle Creek, Michigan. When the Kentucky and Tennessee conference started in 1876, the members were so poor and scattered that collecting tithe from them was difficult, making it hard to sustain ministers in the field.

Without things like jobs, institutions or conferences to offer incentives like financial security or social standing, early Adventism in places like Kentucky and Tennessee had but one advantage: it attracted only believers willing to give up all they had for the sake of truth, a tremendous example of how sacrifice makes the church tick.

Spiritual growth under trying circumstances comes through in the *Review* news stories of Kentucky and Tennessee Adventists between 1865 and 1900. The workers gave attention to public relations and kept their fellow believers in other parts of the country fully informed of their struggles and deprivations.

For example:

An East Tennessee school shut down due to the jailing of the principal and several teachers for violating Sunday laws and later grew into a premier Seventh-day Adventist university.

Burning a tent and firing guns at evangelistic meetings combined with threats to the evangelists in West Tennessee united the believers in purpose and inspired them to build churches and schools. Prominent missionaries as well as other church and conference workers came out of this area.

Jailing new believers for keeping the seventh day and working on the first brought them to their knees and should have finished them off.

Coming out of the Civil War, the southern states were just hard places to labor, especially for people from the detested north, and the people would use the law to silence teachings they were not too sure of.

Yet, people in both states heard the Adventist message by various means and sent out calls for ministers. A representative example of the Adventist literature impact was a testimonial on *Thoughts on Daniel and the Revelation* printed as advertising for the book in the April 8, 1884, edition of the Review and Herald. A Professor D. Moury, principal of the Normal Department at Central Tennessee College wrote that the book "highly pleased" him. "The literature is such that all can readily understand it. It shows the real value of all historical knowledge. It demonstrates beyond any reasonable doubt that the Bible is a book of truth and shows infidelity to be a great mistake. White it is interesting, it is instructive, and as a work of solid worth, it is valuable to us beyond the preciousness of gold. I cannot see how any young man or woman, who has any cultured tastes for history, can afford to be without the knowledge it contains or how any father or mother in this age of knowledge can feel free to allow their children to be ignorant of the living themes with which it is filled. I am glad that it is being circulated among the people, and wish these noble spirits who are circulating it unbounded success."

This book tells the story of how Adventism penetrated many of the smaller towns in Kentucky and Tennessee. Fortunately for history, the early Adventist pioneers had a keen sense of public relations and informed Adventists of their work through sending news stories to the *Review*. Thanks to the Internet and the General Conference of Archives and Statistics, a complete set of Reviews is now easily accessible. By simply writing Kentucky and Tennessee on the search engine, I have uncovered the stories of dedication, sacrifice, persecution and victories among those starting a new religious movement in difficult territory. The hardships seemed to inspire them to keep their faith, and the early churches bore rich fruit.

In addition to the Department of Archives, I also am indebted to Phyllis George, mother of my daughter-in-law, for copy editing this manuscript. She uncovered many mistakes but any remaining are, of course, my responsibility.

Introduction

I thus now send out this book as a tribute to those laying the foundation for what is now the great Kentucky-Tennessee and Georgia Cumberland Conferences. Their work has stood the test of time.

Albert Dittes
Portland, Tennessee
December 23, 2010

The Southern Backdrop

Adventism originated in the abolitionist North, with William Miller and his fellow preachers impacting their native New England. The young movement spread westward through New York, Michigan, Indiana, Ohio and Wisconsin; however, it had but few known believers south of the Mason Dixon Line at the 1863 organization of the General Conference.

The Civil War created bitter divisions in the United States, and at its close in 1865, people in the South had slight interest in anything coming out of the North. This attitude was not lessened by the fact that the *Advent Review and Sabbath Herald* seemed to demonize the South at times. For example, the February 12, 1867, edition of the *Review* ran an article under the title, "Reign of Terror in Tennessee."

"A correspondent of the Cincinnati Gazette writing from Nashville draws the following gloomy picture of the affairs in that State," the article began.

It referred to the recent war as "the rebellion" and said most people in Tennessee still sympathized with it. "Even in the city of Nashville, there is not a day passes in which men are not heard to deplore the downfall of the Confederacy, to curse the Government for overturning it, and to hope for its re-establishment," the author wrote. "Even in the city of Nashville you may traverse the streets as I have done, and you shall not be able to find a dozen portraits of Washington or Lincoln, while in almost every place where any kind of business is transacted, from the wholesale dry goods store to the drinking saloon and the hall of the private boarding house, you shall see conspicuously displayed badly executed and disgusting pictures of Stonewall Jackson and Lee. Even some Union men engaged in business, pitifully yield to the pressure, and exhibit the portraits of men who are known only for a causeless and gigantic effort to destroy their country, and whose infamy, set forth in the pages of impartial history, will make bright by contrast the names of Arnold and Burr."

The correspondent described former slaves as being "oppressed, wronged and outraged to a degree that almost exceeds belief." He said they received no justice from the courts and added that "union men" had it just as hard as the blacks. State legislators loyal to the United States government feared for their lives.

The mistreatment of Negroes clearly fueled the Adventist anti-South bias. A letter published in the June 20, 1868, *Review* told of the recent organization of the Ku Klux Klan in Giles County, Tennessee, painting a terrible picture of it. "One day they take out a white school-teacher, strip him and beat him into a jelly. Another night they warn a radical citizen that his presence in the community is not desired... Again, they go to a Negro's house, take the man out, put a chain about his neck, and mount their horses. The Lost Cause is as dear to them as ever, and what is still more to be wondered at, and what calls for increased vigilance, is the fact that so many in the North now, . . . are urging them on in their unholy work."

Another article that same year said that in Huntington, in Carroll County, Tennessee, the scene of later Adventist persecution, "a Negro woman was taken out and so unmercifully whipped by the Ku-Klux, that for days her back bore bloody testimony to their fiendish cruelty."

Such stories would seem to indicate that Southerners were not the kind of people Adventists would want to be part of their young movement.

"It is established, past all reasonable question, that there prevails an uncontrolled spirit of lawlessness, which continually breaks out into the worst violence and outrage," commented another article in an April 18, 1871, *Review*. "By floggings, expulsions, and murders, a large part of the community in the South are kept in constant terror... Nor, further is it to be denied that at some times and in some sections—as Tennessee and North Carolina—the persecuted party, gaining power, have retaliated with almost equal lawlessness and bitterness upon their foes. But far the greater burden of these sins of violence falls on the enemies of the Negro."

A controversial governor and senator from Tennessee, William Gannaway (Parson) Brownlow, wrote in a letter published in the *Review*, "The rebel party that we are dealing with are as bitter and insulting as they were in 1861, and are as haughty and overbearing as when in the field with arms in their hands. The truth is, this rebel party hate the old flag, and hate the Government of the United States."

Senator Brownlow further accused his political enemies of trying to accomplish through legislation what they had failed to achieve on the battlefield.

Then, a February 17, 1876, edition of the *Review* wrote that Confederate hero Nathan Bedford Forrest would take charge of Negroes under arrest in Memphis, Tennessee, fine them $200, and force them to work it off for him at 25 cents a day, flogging them at night if they didn't process 100 pounds of cotton during the day.

So the Adventist opinion shapers justifiably had serious reservations about southern states like Kentucky and Tennessee after the Civil War.

Nevertheless, the Three Angels' Messages transcended all races, nationalities, and cultures, and therefore found their way South. Some religiously-minded people would find out about Adventism through friends, books, or tracts and write Battle Creek headquarters asking how to become part of this church. Adventist ministers went south and found converts.

The first prominent Adventist minister to work in the South and write about it in against his Adventist faith. Before his apostasy in the 1880's, he visited the South regularly and, like the Apostle Paul in the early days of the New Testament church, shared Adventism with believers, organized them into churches and conferences and grafted them onto the General Conference. His first article appeared in the May 4, 1876, edition of the *Review* was Dudley Marvin (D.M.) Canright who later became notorious for turning *Review,* urging the scattered Kentucky and Tennessee Adventists to assemble at an important gathering to start a new conference. About a month later he wrote from Mammoth Cave, Kentucky, that "In a beautiful grove of large shade trees" on the farm of a Brother David Barr five miles out of Elizabethtown, Kentucky, 35 people representing five churches in two states had organized the Kentucky and Tennessee Conference, comprised of an estimated 100 Sabbath keepers.

"Almost all of them were Southern people; some of them had been slaveholders and rebels during the war, with strong feelings against the Northern people. But now they have laid all these things aside," Canright wrote. "We found them just as warm-hearted, confiding, and true as our Northern people. So far as I can see, they are as ready to hear us and learn the truth from us as though we were Southerners."

Canright sensed an unwillingness of the new white converts to accept their black fellow believers as equals, but felt a good spirit of unity between both races. Each was anxious to reach their native people.

Canright saw possibilities for evangelism there, and spoke of many guests from the community coming out to the meetings. He was particularly pleased to see a Baptist minister named R.G. Garrett embrace Adventism, and hoped he could develop into a valuable helper for Squire Osborn, the only Adventist minister in both states and a natural choice for president. The people elected David Barr as treasurer. Canright represented Kentucky and Tennessee at the 1876 General Conference session in Battle Creek.

Canright described the "poverty and destitution" he saw in Tennessee and Georgia as "distressing," with worn-out soil and idle plantations wherever he went.

"Except in the villages, I did not see a single window or a pane of glass, either in a dwelling house, school house, or meeting house," he wrote. "Carpets, cook stoves, etc., are scarcely known. The people live almost exclusively on pork, coffee and corn bread. Fruit and vegetables are scarcely used at all. Yet almost all kinds of fruit, berries and vegetables will grow in abundance."

Yet in all this Canright saw possibilities for evangelism. "Nearly all the people see that they are making a mistake in this, and say they must change. I am satisfied that it would not be hard to make a change in this respect with those who embrace the truth. Water is abundant and most excellent, and the air is pure and healthful.

"Every man with whom I talked is glad that slavery is no more. All see that it has ruined their country. It has kept down public schools and compelled the great mass to grow up in ignorance. Even now, in the country, they have no schools to amount to anything. All are anxious for Northern men to come among them and show them how to farm, how to have schools, etc."

He noted a great need for education in stewardship. "The churches, except in the cities, contribute almost nothing at all to the support of preaching. Preachers labor for nothing and support themselves, or nearly so. This custom, together with the poverty of the people, must be considered before we send men here to labor. But I am satisfied that there are many honest souls here, and that the present truth is destined soon to make a mighty stir in the South."

Canright's next article, June 15, 1876, described a visit to Tennessee, starting out in Nashville and going east through McMinnville to Bledsoe County. Here Brother Orlando Soule from Michigan had worked six weeks and raised up a company of Sabbath keepers in the "dense, endless forest" comprising the Cumberland Mountains.

Here again, he saw people desiring more truth than what they had. "I find that the whole country around is stirred about this new doctrine, and hundreds are wanting to hear," he wrote. "There are more calls for lectures in different places than can be filled for many months."

Because of the demand for the gospel, Canright ordained Brother Soule "so that he might baptize, organize churches, etc. So at our last meeting, in the midst of his own children in the faith, he was solemnly set apart to the sacred work of the gospel."

Canright sensed no more prejudice to the Three Angels' Messages in the South than he had found in Michigan. He just noted that Kentucky and Tennessee people, especially in the hills, were poorer and less educated than their northern counterparts. They subsisted on cornbread, pork, and coffee, a challenging field to the health reformer. The good news was that wholesome food could be easily raised there.

The next year, Canright called for a four-day conference in Bear Wallow, Hart County, Kentucky. The actual meeting occurred in Powder Mills, about 75 miles south of Louisville.

"Our meeting was a very pleasant one," he wrote in the November 7, 1878, *Review*. "All seemed to be united in fellowship and in confidence in the work. Several made a start to serve God, and nine were baptized. Over $300 was pledged to assist the cause in the State. A lack of means cripples the laborers much as yet but we expect that this will be remedied soon, and that other laborers will be raised up to push on this work. We had an excellent outside interest."

Canright attended the third annual Kentucky and Tennessee Conference meeting in Powder Mills, a session which, having oversight of the Adventist work in Tennessee, ordained G. K. Owen to the ministry. At the 1879 General Conference session, he helped appeal for qualified workers to go south and recommended that they invest their energy more in the cities than in rural areas so as to be at the centers of influence. He also represented the General Conference at the fourth conference session, which, among other things, voted to change the name of the Powder Mills church to Rio and to divide the conference into Kentucky and Tennessee.

"We are glad to find the brethren all in harmony, and hopeful in the work," Canright wrote in the *Review* in summing up the conference session and camp meeting. "There is a good prospect before the cause in this state if more labor can be bestowed here."

He noted that the conference had done well financially but needed to upgrade its accounting practices. It hoped to remedy that situation by sending some of its talented young people to Battle Creek College.

Presiding over the first meeting of the Tennessee Conference in 1879, he reported five small churches and about 75 Sabbath keepers "scattered far and wide."

"Elder Canright spoke of the importance of being in harmony with all the plans of Seventh-day Adventists, and gave valuable instruction about church business, quarterly meetings, etc.," the *Review* report of the meeting stated. "Nearly all are poor people, and hence the cause is still weak."

He left Brother G.K. Owen and his wife in charge of the Tennessee believers and again noted the stewardship need. "They have labored faithfully and well, with little remuneration," he wrote. "This should be remembered when the Conference is stronger. . . There are many harder fields than Tennessee. Experienced, persevering labor will certainly build up a good work here."

Canright also presided over the organization of a Temperance Society and the Sabbath School Association in Kentucky.

Squire Osborn, the first president of the Kentucky and Tennessee conference, acknowledged in a *Review* article the hostile feelings lingering between North and South after settling the political differences. Addressing primarily his constituents, he wrote, "Many of our brethren have had strong Southern principles. They are as honest and sincere as any one; but unless we crucify these feelings entirely, and regard our Northern brethren as our true friends and Christian brethren, in times of trial and temptation these old differences will take root again and grow up, will separate us from God and his people, and drown our souls in perdition."

He then reminded them of the help from Battle Creek and not to stereotype Yankees as being all bad.

"As it regards the interest that our Northern brethren have for the South, and their love for us, I need only remark: They have not stood still and simply prayed for us. They have given us the best evidence of their fidelity by donating to us $292 to purchase a tent to be used in these States, and by sending us one of their ablest counselors to attend our first Conference. It is also probable that they will send Bro. George I. Butler to labor in this Conference this season. They ask no remuneration from us. Our Conference is weak, and we need help, and they have shown that they are friends indeed by helping us in our time of need. This should satisfy us that they have no feeling against us. They have shown by their works that they believe this message is one—a world-wide message;--whether, east, west, north or south it is the same. O my brethren, let us ever act in full union and harmony with them. One more word under this head. The atmosphere of the North seems to give life and activity to the people, while that of the South seems to produce lassitude and inactivity. Here is where we should press a little. 'Be zealous and repent,' says the True Witness."

Another prominent Adventist leader to take a serious interest in the South was James White. As president of the General Conference in 1876, he saw annual camp meetings as "gatherings of great importance" and wanted to extend them into newly developing fields such as Virginia, Kentucky, Texas and other Southern states.

"That there are strong sectional feelings between the people of the North and the people of the South, no one acquainted with the history of our country will deny," he wrote in the Dec. 9, 1880, *Review*. "What political prejudice and narrow selfishness have not done to bring about this state of things, may be set down in the account of ignorance of the character and real feelings of the people North and South."

White then pointed out that his New England background had rendered him antislavery, a viewpoint the Civil War had magnified. Pioneering Adventist work in California brought him into direct contact with Southern people for the first time.

He wrote that pictures of great Southern personalities like Jefferson Davis, Robert E. Lee or Stonewall Jackson in the homes of people he visited "were at first as repulsive to our feelings as the presence of a colored man with white men at the table, or in the house of God, is to one whose birth and education have been in the South."

"But these persons who had moved from the South to California with Southern principles and feelings, and had there given their hearts to the Lord to keep all his commandments, were excellent people; and by associating with them, both they and we seemed to forget that the habits of both were formed in different latitudes."

His California experience with Southerners enabled him to work successfully in Texas two years later. While the news media there had run articles misrepresenting Adventists, White made it clear that the people writing them were not speaking for the church, and he had found the Texas editors to be people of quality and integrity.

So he saw no reason to exclude Southerners from Seventh-day Adventism. "We would say to all our dear brethren in the South, The cause is one. You have the confidence and sympathy of your brethren in the North. 'Let there be no strife between us; for we are brethren.'"

The Conference Founders

A Quick Overview

The first Seventh-day Adventist to write in the *Review* about Tennessee was a minister from the north named E.B. Lane. He conducted meetings in a railroad station near Nashville called Edgefield Junction.

"Here are a few keeping the Sabbath who desire baptism," he wrote in the May 2, 1871 *Review*. "They embraced the truth from reading publications, having never heard a discourse from one of our ministers."

In the railroad depot, black people sat in one room and whites in another in accordance with the Jim Crow segregation laws of the time. These meetings actually resulted in a company of 13 members, which evolved during the next century into the present Nashville First SDA Church. Brother R.K. McCune, another missionary-minded Adventist from the North, worked in Tennessee for awhile before moving back to Wisconsin. "We are very anxious that he should return," wrote Mary A. Remley in the July 15, 1875, edition of the *Review*. "We believe he could do much good here, as he was the first to introduce the truth in our vicinity."

She added that his work, with the assistance of two visits from Brother E.B. Lane, had resulted in 17 people keeping the Sabbath. "We have Sabbath-keepers in

East, West and Middle Tennessee," she wrote. "Is not that some inducement for a preacher to come to this State?"

Squire Osborn, a talented speaker with a knack for hard work, became the minister to answer this call. He had moved from Greenup County, Kentucky, to the Iowa territory at the age of 26, accepted the Adventist faith there, and returned home with his wife Mary in 1871. From then on, he preached the Adventist message, some in Tennessee but mostly in Kentucky.

Osborn would receive letters saying, "I've been reading a tract from the Adventists, and I believe it is right. How do I get into this church?" He would travel to meet with these interested parties, conduct meetings, and baptize new converts, then repeat the process in another place; but meanwhile, new converts all over the region had no organized churches to go to and limited pastoral help.

Because he was at times the only minister in both states, he had too much territory to cover. It is hard to remain a church member when there is no church, and it is equally difficult to create a church where the members are widely scattered and no pastor exists. Nevertheless some, no matter how isolated, kept the faith. His dispatches to the *Review* showed him doing the best he could with what he had despite persecution, backsliding and a lack of funds.

For example, in the August 5, 1875, *Review*, Osborn briefly summed up his work in Hammonville, Hart County, Kentucky. "I have stopped labor here for the present, as the rain breaks up our meeting nearly every night. I think I will wait until the weather is more favorable. I have had good attendance when the weather would admit of it, notwithstanding the prejudice. I am about two-thirds through with a course of lectures, and four have taken their stand on the Sabbath. There are a few more that are investigating. I will try to visit the brethren in Tennessee. Brother E.B. Lane wrote, requesting me to do so if it was possible."

The Glasgow, Kentucky *Times* described Squire Osborn as "a man of more than ordinary ability" in a report of meetings he conducted in Edmonton in 1877.

"Thoroughly schooled in every rule of his faith, he walks forth upon the broad field of debate, and while standing in the very center of scriptural controversy, he analyzes with easy effort the most difficult problems. And with beautiful consistency he harmonizes scriptures which appear to be plain contradictions, and which have puzzled and vexed the stoutest energies of the most learned in Bible teaching in our whole community. . . To have him go from our midst is not our choice; but we hope wherever he may pitch his tent circumstances may bless him, as they have done here, with large and attentive crowds throughout his entire series of lectures."

Osborn chronicled his work in great detail through the pages of the *Review*. His dispatches reveal a busy ministry in a difficult, seemingly unpromising area.

Starting Out

He organized the first church in Kentucky at Locust Grove in Hardin County, in 1873. Other early scenes of his labors were Ohio County, Knob Lick in Metcalfe County, Edmonton, Hoods Run, Catalpa Grove in Green County, and Greenup along the Ohio River.

"This is out of my State (Kentucky), but it seemed duty to come here," he wrote about Pleasant View, Tennessee, in the January 20, 1876, edition of the *Review*. "There are now nine here keeping the Sabbath."

At a specially-called meeting of the General Conference in April of 1876, he reported five organized churches in Kentucky and two in Tennessee. The Battle Creek brethren promised to give him a tent for holding evangelistic meetings.

He then preached in Hodgenville, LaRue County, Kentucky, birthplace of Abraham Lincoln; and advertised a camp meeting in Elizabethtown, Hardin County, at the home of David Barr.

"We have now been at this place three weeks," Osborn reported from Bear Wallow near Horse Cave, Kentucky. "The interest is still good, the congregations averaging from 150 to 250. The whole country for miles around is being stirred. We have canvassed the Sabbath question fully; and several have commenced its observance. Books sell quite freely."

A mildew-proof tent turned out to be a valuable tool there, with several people keeping the Sabbath. The local clergy complained some but gave no open opposition.

His final 1876 dispatch came from Powder Mills, a town that would become an important center for early Adventism in Kentucky. While the Bear Wallow converts had apparently kept the faith; Osborn found the Powder Mills people, on the other hand, receptive but slow to act. "Therefore much labor is needed to perfect them in the work."

Back to Tennessee

The demands of the infant work next took him to the struggling group in Edgefield Junction, Tennessee. He also met with believers in the Robertson County community of Coopertown, making his temporary headquarters nearby in Pleasant View in neighboring Cheatham County. Brother G.K. Owen from Michigan joined him there and became a great help with his singing talent. He left with six people keeping the Sabbath and many more in the community acknowledging Adventism as the true faith.

A Brother Orlando Soule stayed behind to follow up the interest as Squire Osborn moved on to Elizabethtown, Kentucky. Here he and fellow believers decided to conduct a camp meeting back at Bear Wallow, Kentucky. "Brother D.M. Canright is strongly urged and expected to attend," he wrote in the May 3, 1877 *Review*.

"Elder S. Osborn of Kentucky has been with us several days," wrote James White in the May 31, 1877 edition of the *Review*. "He reports a membership in the Kentucky and Tennessee Conference of seventy, and

160 Sabbath keepers within the bounds of his mission... Brother Osborn is one of our hard-working, faithful men. If it pleases God, Mrs. White and I will hold a camp meeting with his people in late autumn."

Keeping the poor and scattered people on track proved difficult. "For a month previous to our camp meeting, I was engaged in visiting the churches and scattered brethren and sisters," he wrote in the May 31, 1877, *Review*. "I found most of them in a backslidden state. Some of them were still clinging to their idols, notwithstanding they had promised to quit them. Coffee, pork, and tobacco are among the staple articles of food in the State."

Osborn hoped for revival at camp meeting, and had a good representation from Tennessee, including a school headmaster from Coopertown Institute, in Robertson County. He assigned Brother Orlando Soule to oversee the Tennessee work and found two good people to assist him in Kentucky.

Osborn reported in the *Review* that they admitted the Mount Gilead church into the conference, making six churches and 67 members in Kentucky during the first half of 1877. With this many churches, he needed more pastoral help!

Squire Osborn received $230.65 for his labors during the previous year, but Orlando Soule was paid only $55.

With camp meeting over, Osborn conducted meetings in Glover's Creek. But a most important matter demanded his attention: he was asked to preside at the marriage ceremony of Orlando Soule to Miss Alice Turner. Next he went on to Powder Mills and back to the Elizabethtown home of D.W. Barr, one of his strong supporters.

His Work Bore Fruit

A Brother J.T.Y. Crockett of Lincoln County, Kentucky wrote in the *Review*, "About a year ago I first met Brother S. Osborn, and had the Sabbath question brought before my mind. Since that time I have carefully and prayerfully examined the proof and thank God that in his providence I met Brother Osborn. It looks surprising to me that I never saw or rather never understood the plain teachings of God's word in regard to the seventh day before." Brother Crockett withdrew from the Cumberland Presbyterian Church where he had served as preacher for several years.

Osborn went to Shepherdsville on March 14, 1878, and would wind up making that community his home and burial spot. According to his news clip in the *Review*, he went there at the request of several Sabbath keepers he had worked with the year before and found to his surprise much of the prejudice from his past venture all gone. "The schoolhouse that holds about a hundred, is now crammed every evening," he wrote. "I have been preaching day and night to the present, but my strength is not sufficient to hold out that way any longer."

Starting More Churches

His travels took him to a quarterly meeting in Elizabethtown, a short series of meetings in Bear Wallow, then on to organize a 10-member church at Glover's Creek. "I found the Sabbath-keepers here had given up pork, coffee, and tobacco, and were ready for organization," he wrote.

He next organized a church in Bullitt County and went on to Tennessee to find a spot for evangelism in Goodlettsville. "We commenced meetings here in the tent under very unfavorable circumstances; but prejudice is giving way and increasing interest is manifest," he wrote. "The attendance has not been very large, but our audiences have been composed of the best class of citizens, and the best of attention is given."

The meetings continued with increasing interest, but in the end, he baptized only three people, two of whom had kept the Sabbath before.

Osborn next went to Cross Plains, Tennessee, where he would leave a lasting mark. "This pleasant village 12 miles from the railroad contains about 125 inhabitants," he reported. "They are very kind in supplying our needs. We have large congregations of attentive hearers. Books sell."

The next *Review* dispatch from Tennessee told of a Sunday evening congregation of 500 people with a reduced interest due to the introduction of the Sabbath plus "dark nights and rainy weather." "We know of only six who have decided to keep the Sabbath," he wrote. "As is usually the case in this state, the majority are convinced, and there they stand."

He stayed with the Cross Plains converts, however, later learning of 16 people keeping the Sabbath there, and then called for a Kentucky rally in Powder Mills.

Squire Osborn represented Kentucky and Tennessee at the 17th annual session of the General Conference in Battle Creek in the fall of 1878. Later on that year, the third annual session of the Kentucky and Tennessee Conference at Powder Mills admitted the Glovers Creek church into the conference.

An end-of-year supplement to the *Review* showed the Tennessee Conference contributing $6.90 towards the Dime Tabernacle in Battle Creek, with 60 cents of that coming from Squire Osborn.

Osborn counted 50 Sabbath-keepers from six Kentucky counties attending a June, 1879, quarterly meeting. At Slick Rock a few weeks later, he told of three people keeping the Sabbath, but "persecution is beginning to rage against them in the form of ridicule, which seems to be a powerful argument." A few Sabbath keepers lived in Sulphur Springs. At that point, Kentucky had one minister--Squire Osborn—and five churches, with a total of 54 members.

Splitting One Conference into Two

At the fourth annual session of the Kentucky and Tennessee Conference in October of 1879, the constituency decided to divide the conference in two, leaving Squire Osborn with only one state to cover. G.K. Owen took charge of the Tennessee Conference. They also changed the name of the Powder Mills Church to Rio.

D.M. Canright attended this meeting and reported a good spirit in his *Review* account, but noted that while the Kentucky finances had improved, they had added another worker, R.G. Garrett, to assist Brother Osborn and therefore needed more money.

Highs and Lows in Kentucky

Osborn next worked fruitfully in Hardin County, stirring up the Methodist neighborhood by teaching the state of the dead.

In Litchfield, Grayson County, Kentucky, he found the people "still addicted to injurious practices. I tried to set before them their practical duties especially in reference to the tithing system, and to impress on them the importance of the *Testimonies to the Church*. They were all satisfied that we have the truth on these points, but it seemed hard for them to give up all for Christ."

Prospects looked brighter in Custer, Breckenridge County. "They heartily endorse every point of our faith. They are wanting baptism, preparatory to church organization, and this will be attended to sometime in April. A Sabbath school was organized, and the tithing system adopted. All have quit the use of coffee, pork, and tobacco. I spent five days here in debate with a Baptist minister on the Sabbath, the first day, and the nature of man. He challenged me while I was holding a meeting." The debate resulted in a victory for the truth. "To God be all the praise."

Regarding Seatonsville in Jefferson County, "I have never had a more promising field of labor than this."

Unfortunately, the Summer Shade Church dropped four members. But on a more positive note, evangelistic meetings in Big Spring, Breckenridge County attracted a large attendance.

At "one of the largest gatherings of Sabbath keepers we have ever had in the State," a quarterly meeting at Shepherdsville in 1880, "many of our people are isolated, and these are the only meetings they can attend; hence they prize such privileges highly."

After meetings at Cross Roads, he wrote of a healthy interest but hard-to-gauge results. "In the South it takes at least twice the labor to get the people fully into the truth that it does in the North." In 1881, ministerial travels took Osborn to places like Seatonsville, Bowling Green and Knob Lick.

Duty Calls Him Back to Struggling Tennessee

The departure of Brother Owen had caused morale to sag. He resolved some of the difficulties in Essex Junction, the Ridge church in Cheatham County, and Cross Plains. Backsliding continued to be a serious problem. He also warned his people in both states about a traveling man claiming to be "the second John the Baptist" with a form of Adventism masquerading as "new light."

By now, Osborn was operating out of Shepherdsville, Kentucky, just south of Louisville. He would spend nine weeks at a time away from home making the Kentucky pastoral circuit, and hope in vain that the General Conference would send more ministerial help to Tennessee. In the meantime, some Tennessee believers would hopefully attend a camp meeting in Elizabethtown.

Osborn found the Cross Plains and Cheatham County Ridge churches going through serious trials. A new church of 11 members in Springville, Henry County in West Tennessee met only every other Sabbath, but eight days of meetings and visitation seemed to revive spirits there. Edgefield Junction was down in membership and morale. Osborn just had too much territory to cover.

Problem of Underserving the Members

"I see more than ever the importance and the necessity of feeding the sheep and lambs," he wrote concerning his overload. "They must be taken care of. It is not good generalship to press our work into the enemy's camp, and leave the rear unprotected. While we may take some prisoners, we lose our tried soldiers."

Four churches sent delegates to the 1881 Tennessee Conference in Cross Plains. The *Review* report listed Springville and Edgefield Junction as being present. The Ridge Church in Cheatham County was presumably the other one.

After the 1881 death of Adventist pioneer James White, the Kentucky Conference honored him by saying, "that while we deeply deplore his loss, we recognize the hand of God in the bright and shining works which do follow him; and we are thankful for the example of his life of consecration, pointing out the way in which the living may bless their fellow-men and glorify God."

At the 1881 General Conference session, also mourning the death of James White, the Committee on Destitute Fields recommended that Elder Samuel Fulton of Minnesota help Osborn in Tennessee.

Osborn met him and J.Q. Finch of West Tennessee in Nashville, and he seemed to think their visit helped the five believers there, whom he described as being "in rather a low condition." He also introduced Fulton to the Edgefield Junction believers and took him east to the discouraged believers in the Cumberland Mountains. The Ridge Church remained backslidden.

Osborn once again devoted himself to his native Kentucky, organizing a meeting in Metcalf County, but still conducted meetings in Springville, Tennessee as president of the Tennessee Conference, having spent four months away from home working there with Elder Fulton.

Back to Concentrating on Kentucky

Believers from Elizabethtown, Rio, Custer, Summershade, and Seatonsville composed a quarterly meeting in Metcalfe County, Kentucky.

Osborn reported good interest in Normandy, (Spencer County), Union Star and Glascow. Tennessee had a good news/bad news situation. Cross Plains seemed to be growing, but Edgefield Junction and Ridge "had drawn back to perdition."

Osborn had a hard time in Franklin Cross Roads, Harden County, Kentucky, during the summer of 1882, but he marveled that the four Sabbath keepers in his native Greenup County had stayed faithful for five years "having no preacher but the *Review*." Seatonsville, Rio and Elizabethtown sent good representations to the quarterly meeting. "I can say for Kentucky, though in the hot-bed of tobacco raising, there is not a member in all our ranks who uses the filthy weed, and only two outside Sabbath-keepers who are addicted to the habit; but nearly all used it when they heard present truth."

At Vine Grove in the summer of 1882, everything seemed against him. "The people have been drunk with the leaven of politics, and some whisky," he wrote. "Though the election is over, the influence is not gone."

A bumper crop of wheat and competing meetings by the Baptists also took people away, as did an entertaining phrenology lecturer nearby.

Hard Work Paying Off

Prominent Adventist minister George I. Butler wrote highly of Squire Osborn in the *Review*. "Brother Osborn has labored faithfully, and we know that God has helped him. But he feels the need of helpers who can go into larger places, and reach the intelligent classes. No doubt it is more difficult to bring people out of the worldly influences which are around them in the South than in the North."

Backsliding again surfaced as the real problem at the January, 1883, quarterly meeting at Rio. The people wanted to do better. They were so scattered that the meeting passed a resolution asking "that each member now present shall urge the members of their respective churches to report in person or by letter to the elders of our churches at each regular church meeting."

Osborn pressed on to Nolin, Custer, and Garfield in Breckenridge County, even though his two-year-old granddaughter died in 1883. A prominent minister came to speak against him in Garfield, but two people later started keeping the Sabbath despite it. Scattered church members attending a quarterly meeting in Mount Washington encouraged the two Sabbath keepers there and made a positive impact in the community.

The eighth annual session of the Kentucky Conference, held in Glasgow, asked for the General Conference to send them a minister for at least one year, "and we will do our utmost by our means and prayers to sustain him." The session also asked for Ellen White to attend the camp meeting next year.

He went on to Pelleville in Hancock County and West Clifty, and then shared some good news with his people through the *Review* in the spring of 1884.

Help from the North Finally on the Way

"Dear brethren we have been crippled heretofore for the want of means and help in the ministry; by the blessing of God we are to be supplied this season with both," Osborn wrote. "Ohio has come to our relief. Her arms of sympathy have been extended to us and have placed the means within our reach, providing we take hold of the work, and by doing our duty show ourselves worthy of help."

G.G. Rupert, president of the Ohio Conference, answered the Macedonian call to Kentucky. He announced in the *Review* that he was moving his family to Battle Creek so his wife could get needed treatments in the Sanitarium, and that he himself had moved to Kentucky to labor for the church and to work the territory by selling books, starting in Horse Cave and Nolin. He noted two men already canvassing Bowling Green. "The brethren in Kentucky appreciate the help sent from Ohio, and are going to try to make the most of it," he wrote.

He then presided over a state meeting in West Clifty and started a series of meetings in Glasgow.

Osborn meanwhile had a good experience in the Hancock County community of Pleasant Zion, selling publications, collecting offerings, and even benefiting from the opposition of a prominent Baptist debater. He also went to Boston in Nelson County and then by request to nearby Nelsonville.

The ninth annual session of the Kentucky Conference in October, 1884, presided over by Osborn, disbanded the Seatonville Church but recognized new companies at West Clifty, Nelsonville and Pleasant Zion. They appointed G.C. Rupert to represent the state at the General Conference and asked for several pledges, one of them being "$500 to pay indebtedness to the ministers."

Mob Violence

Osborn's first 1886 report to the Review makes exciting reading.

"I began to hold meetings in the Anti-Baptist church in the vicinity of some 10 Sabbath keepers on the evening of December 11, and continued until the evening of the 16th," he began. "During that time I heard a number of times that a mob was going to 'run me out of the country.' We had a good outside interest, and I had no confidence in such news, as reports of this kind are so common everywhere we go. But just before our meeting closed, the report was circulated among the congregation that the mob was outside the door. After the service, Brother Hardin invited me to go home with him, to do which we would have to go a mile through the woods, with only three of us. But, as I believe, a good providence directed a Brother Gardner (Baptist) to ask me to his home.

"After we had started, a friend told us that the mob were near, and intended to follow me. Still, I hardly believed it, and went on with Brother Gardner. When we had gone about 300 yards from the house, two men ran ahead of me and, wheeling round, caught hands, and commanded me to halt. I demanded their business with me, when I saw I was entirely surrounded by a drunken, angry mob. Brother Gardner stepped into the ring, placed his hand on the shoulder of the leader, and commanded him in the name of the commonwealth of the State, and as a citizen of that county, not to lay hands on me. One of the men drew his revolver, asking if he took up for me; if so, he would shoot him or any other man that would do it. Brother Gardner said he had invited me home with him, and he meant to protect me. The man stood with cocked pistol and Brother Gardner between me and him. I was satisfied he did not intend to shoot him; but I was the object of their vengeance, and so with all the authority I could command I said, 'Men, stand back, and let me pass,' which they did. They seemed to be held in check by some unseen power. My friend was holding the leader at bay, but, offering to fight if it became necessary, they started after me again, and said with a horrid oath that they would accomplish their object. They stopped, however, although they threatened to carry out their project. Some citizens came in, and after consulting together, we decided to have them arrested. The court advised me not to go back the next night unless the officers could get there to protect me. If I had gone, there would have been a fight; for both sides went there armed.

"The next day four of the desperadoes were arrested. Their trial lasted two days. The leader, Jackson, was fined $50 and costs and given 10 days in jail. The rest were bound over to circuit court under bonds of $200 each. If they keep out of the penitentiary, it will not cost them less than $600. No sect is responsible for this; it was simply a drunken mob. When the trial was over, I went back and finished up my meetings unmolested, baptizing two willing souls."

"Severe trials" had afflicted the Glasgow and Summer Shade churches by the summer of 1886, but Osborn's visit hopefully revived them, according to his dispatch. By that year, Bowling Green, Russellville and Madisonville had organized churches, again plagued by apostasy "and the moving malady." The same could be said for Providence, Marion and Dalton. Ministers had conducted meetings in these places and found converts, but discouragement seemed to set in after they left.

He found two people in Auburn, Kentucky, "alive in the truth, though alone." Bridgeport and Alvaton in Warren County felt his influence.

"I can truly say that the Lord is blessing his cause here," he wrote in the February 20, 1884 edition of the *Review*. "There are now 20 white native Sabbath-keepers, four of whom are men, and many others who are deeply interested." Money was also coming in well. The next year he reported six new believers as a result of the work of Joseph Collie and Charles Kilgore.

Osborn's health started slipping about this time, and he did not write another article for the *Review* until 1893. Then he reported progress among the whites in Louisville near his Shepherdsville home, with 13 people taking their stand for the Sabbath and four being baptized in the Ohio River.

In 1898, Osborn reported that Louisville church membership was up, but membership in Rio, one of the early churches he had raised up 25 years before, had gone down. "The church at that place had been much reduced by removals, apostasies, and deaths. But few of the old members are left; and their families have grown up to manhood and womanhood since I was there."

Yet he found one of the pioneers in Hart County, a Sister Forrest, still strong in the faith, though isolated and now widowed.

Squire Osborn continued visiting the Kentucky churches and entering new fields,

The Squire Osborn grave in Cedar Grove Cemetery near Shepherdsville, Kentucky. News stories spelled his last name without the "e."

Squire and Mary Osborn share the same plot.

dying in the summer of 1903 at the age of 78 after attending an eastern Kentucky camp meeting.

"He fell at his post, with his armor on," commented his *Review* obituary. "Paralysis of the heart was the immediate cause of his death, but we felt that the Lord had honored his aged servant by laying him away amid the happiest scenes of his later life."

Pioneer ministers like Squire Osborn and Orlando Soule may have lacked what it took to make the opinion shapers in the metropolitan areas feel their influence, but they worked hard in the smaller places and got results. Other Adventist ministers came during the 19th century and attracted more attention in the *Review*, but they at least had something to start with. Osborn's work showed that people in the backward, tobacco-smoking, Negro-hating south would accept Adventism. Those laboring after him found converts among both blacks and whites.

Other Early workers

While early Kentucky and Tennessee Adventists could barely afford to pay Squire Osborn, other ministers heard and answered the Macedonian call. They worked at great sacrifice, and the Lord blessed their efforts.

One of the earliest to join Squire Osborn was Orlando Soule, 26 years old and a new convert at the time of his first appearance in the *Review* pages in 1876. According to his *Review* obituary, Elder J.N. Andrews had baptized him the day before going to Europe as the first Adventist overseas worker in 1874. Soule attended Battle Creek College and then went to Tennessee.

Squire Osborn described him in May of 1877 as "willing to work, and if he keeps humble, God will make him a useful man in this cause."

Soule began in Bledsoe County and wrote, "Urgent invitations are coming from all directions for labor. Eight neighborhoods now stand anxiously waiting for their turn to come. The Sequatchee Valley is from three to five miles wide and 65 miles long, and as far as heard from, the people are all awake to hear. I am now at Pikeville, a little village situated a little above the middle of this valley; having held two meetings with a very good attendance. Brethren, pray that the Spirit of God may set the truth home to men's hearts in this long-neglected part of the vineyard."

He got little response in Pikeville but found many families in other places willing to listen to him. A visit from D.M. Canright was a big help. Writing from Bee Creek, Soule at least had a Sabbath Bible class going.

But when the Lord worked, the devil replied with a vengeance. "About the time of my last report, word was circulated that I must leave the country or I would be disposed of some other way, and then Sabbath-keepers would have to give up their foolish notions, as they are called, or they would share the same fate," he wrote in the August 17, 1876, edition of the *Review*. "All things considered, I thought it my duty to remain with the brethren until things were quieter. One Sunday, while at a private house writing, and knowing nothing of it until it was past, a mob, composed of professors and worldlings, visited a house of worship where they thought to find me. Being disappointed, they inquired for me, and were told that I was at another place, three and a half miles away. They immediately repaired thither through a drenching rain, to be again disappointed. If men will do such things now, without the sanction of law, what may

Sabbath-keepers expect in the near future, when the laws will be framed to uphold these opposers in their work?"

The mob apparently dispersed, but an ague sickness detained him in that community longer than he had intended.

Soule tried again near Glade Creek, Tennessee, retaining his Pikeville address, and found several responding favorably to the Sabbath question despite adverse circumstances. "Opposition has been organized and determined," he wrote. "The learned man that was called in conducted himself so badly that he scarcely needed reviewing; and that having failed, they organized the stay-away club, and nearly all joined it."

Soule did not identify "the learned man" but indicated his presentation may have been self-defeating.

"A few, however, were interested, so I have continued the effort; and now the attention of the unconverted is arrested, and eight have signified their intention to become Christians," he concluded.

He baptized three people there.

Fifty miles distant a group of Sabbath keepers requested his services. Soule walked the entire distance, then held nine meetings and organized a church. He stayed in Bledsoe County, listing his address at Nine Miles.

Soule's next stop was Nashville. Finding the believers there had apparently moved, he looked towards conducting meetings in Franklin. Adventism in Tennessee just seemed to move slowly as 1877 started. He worked briefly with Squire Osborn, whom he found "refreshing," and next reported giving 38 lectures somewhere and knowing of six people keeping the Sabbath. Pickings seemed slim in Edgefield Junction, Ridge, Sycamore Mills and Coopertown. At Union Chapel, ten people signed a covenant to keep the Ten Commandments, including a local deacon who happened to be justice of the peace, local elder, and county surveyor.

Soule must have worked at great personal sacrifice: the May, 1877, quarterly meeting report showed him being paid only $5, while Squire Osborn received $230.65.

By the summer of that year, he could report the largest gathering of its kind ever convened in Tennessee, with a total of 35 Sabbath-keepers from the Edgefield Junction, Union Chapel and Ridge churches. He then conducted some meetings in Lebanon and asked for help in the August 9, 1877 *Review*.

"Young men, read this," Soule proclaimed. "There are hundreds of men in the South raising the Macedonian cry, 'Come over and help us.' Experienced laborers are needed, to be sure; but there is probably no other place in our country in which beginners could gain an experience in presenting the truth better than in the South.

"In nearly every part of Tennessee, lonely Sabbath-keepers are calling for help. Some of them have been calling for four or five years."

Church-building was not the only matter on Brother Soule's mind, however. He had come to know a young lady named Alice Turner, a new convert. Acquaintance ripened into friendship and friendship into love. The two were married by Squire Osborn as part of a series of evangelistic meetings in Glover's Creek, Kentucky, on September 23, 1877.

But even romance could not distract this man from soul-winning. He "labored from house to house" there, and then went to find a discouraged group in Edmonton, Kentucky. "I remained two days, and spoke seven times," he wrote. "All seemed encouraged. Six more signed the covenant. Temporary leaders were appointed, and regular Sabbath meetings will be held."

Back in Tennessee, Soule went to Old Center, two miles away from Edgefield Junction, then back to Edgefield, feeling the need of more help in working Nashville, the capital of Tennessee. "Nashville has nearly 50,000 inhabitants," he wrote. "There is a city library, free to all, where they offer to take Adventist books for the benefit of the many readers. Who will send our workers to this city?"

He seemed to have better luck at Eaton's Creek, with all but three families there "acknowledging the truth." He also sensed possibilities at Simpkins Chapel, but his new converts there faced great family opposition.

Working with Squire Osborn in Glovers Creek, Kentucky, seemed profitable, with 400 people coming out to their meeting to hear two Sabbath message sermons. They held their audience despite challenges from religious groups called Disciples and Universalists.

Then in Tennessee, his *Review* dispatch on June 13, 1878, found him helping the Union Chapel believers. The Mt. Gilead church was going through a down cycle, and he planned to operate out of Edgefield Junction in 1878.

Orlando Soule died in 1940 at Lake Worth, Florida. "After completing his education, he preached the message for 50 years," his obituary stated. "His last active years of service were spent in Tennessee."

G.K. Owen

During the hard winter of 1876-77, Orlando Soule "counseled with the brethren regarding exchanging the mud of the country for the pavements of city or town." His superiors directed him to look up an "unorganized" company in Nashville. When he arrived there, Soule found the people in the church had moved away, but he did meet a missionary-minded Adventist from Michigan named G.K. Owen, who would prove useful in keeping alive the infant Adventist movement in Tennessee.

After much thought and prayer, Soule and Owen decided to hold meetings in nearby Franklin, Tennessee. Squire Osborn left his busy Kentucky ministry to help encourage them, and a month later, in the February 22, 1877, *Review*, he wrote highly of Brother Owen. Osborn had found a fine class of people open to Advent teachings in the Robertson County community of Coopertown. Brother Owen had the gift of music, and organized some of the people into a choir. He rehearsed them an hour before meeting time and broke down prejudice with good singing.

Osborn helped Brother Owen start a series of meetings in Sycamore Mills, Tennessee, before returning to Kentucky. Owen apparently had good results there as well as at Union Chapel.

He wrote of preaching 16 sermons at Center Point. His brief account indicated some trouble in that "we were requested to withdraw our appointments. We then visited from house to house. Six are keeping the Sabbath. Many others acknowledge its obligation, but think they must go with the majority."

Then in Coopertown, he wrote, "Three more have commenced to keep the Sabbath. Dr. Glover has been lecturing against the Sabbath, claiming that the moral law is all typical and was all abolished at the death of Christ. We tried, with the help of the Lord, to present the nature and claims of his law, Sunday evening. The church was crowded with attentive hearers."

At Turnersville, also in Robertson County, he preached in a Methodist Church, and wrote that local pastoral opposition helped more than hurt him.

Brother Owen worked with Squire Osborn at Goodlettsville, made headway against prejudice, and built a substantial congregation of hearers. While many people agreed with them, most found it hard to actually keep the Sabbath, and they baptized only three people. They then started a Cross Plains group in 1878, with 16 people initially keeping the Sabbath and facing opposition.

Brother Owen followed through with his work in Cross Plains and reported 15 more Sabbath keepers and more calls to lecture than he could fill. He crossed the Kentucky state line into Simpson County and found a good interest there but listed his address at Black Jack in Robertson County, Tennessee, and also kept up his work in Turnersville.

The third annual Conference session in 1878 voted to ordain G.K. Owen to the ministry and grant him credentials as well as to appoint him to oversee Adventist work in Tennessee.

Finding new converts was still hard. "We have held meetings in three different school houses since the Kentucky Conference," he wrote early in 1879. "The people admit the truth almost unanimously, but only a few have the moral courage to do what they know and acknowledge to be their duty."

He found a Cheatham County church in Paradise Ridge "in a very critical condition" and experienced backlash from the community when he tried to revive things. "After our meetings commenced, a mob spirit was aroused, and threats were made to stop us before the end of the week, or lay the church in ashes; but an unseen Hand stilled the tempest, and we have since had good order and interested congregations, notwithstanding bad roads and bad weather," he wrote. "This is a hard field, and without the help of the Lord and the abiding presence of his Holy Spirit, our efforts will be in vain; therefore pray for us."

He then went to Henry County in early 1879 and found a good response in Springville, a scene where in the future, believers would face indictments, jail sentences, and loss of productivity.

Initially he found five people keeping the Sabbath at the start of his meetings but immediately ran into what he called bitter and determined opposition.

"Five ministers have exposed the weakness of their own positions; first, by several of them refusing to converse on the subject of the Sabbath, even when asked for instruction; second, by forbidding the preaching of any more strange doctrine in the Methodist Church; third by several opposition discourses, which were reviewed; fourth, last Sabbath a Methodist minister sent a constable to serve a writ on three of our brethren, for breaking the Sabbath on Sunday, May 25. They refused to transact any business with the officer on the Sabbath, and we persuaded him to go with us to the meeting."

The constable was so impressed with what he heard that he sided with the Adventists.

"Yesterday I attended the trial at the court house," Owen continued. "Two of our brethren were acquitted at once, as no testimony was brought against them. The minister was charged with the entire cost."

Owen baptized seven people in Springville and organized a 20-member Sabbath School in the summer of 1879. Panic from a yellow fever epidemic in Memphis sidelined him, but he ordained Brother J.H. Dortch as a local elder for Springville at a quarterly meeting at Edgefield Junction in addition to baptizing several people there as well.

The 1879 session of the Kentucky and Tennessee Conference voted to split into two separate entities, with Tennessee electing Owen as president.

"Brother G.K. Owen and wife have had the oversight of the work in the State the past year, and will have still," wrote D.M. Canright in the *Review* after the first Tennessee Conference meeting. "They have labored faithfully and well, with little remuneration. This should be remembered when the Conference is stronger."

The two states stayed closely associated, organizing a temperance society with Owen as president and Belle Campbell of Elizabethtown, Kentucky, as secretary.

With 33 members, Tennessee was the second smallest conference in North America, according to a quarterly report ending April 1, 1880. Virginia bottomed out the list with 13 members. Kentucky was the third smallest, with 84 members, just four less than Dakota.

Owen's missionary work ultimately took him to India. He died there in 1912, according to his obituary, living near his daughter, the wife of a pioneer worker there.

Patrick D. Moyers

An early Adventist convert to follow up Soule's work was P.D. Moyers, according to dispatches he wrote for the *Review* during the course of several years. He first did so in Cumberland County after Soule and Owen left to conduct their meetings in Franklin, Tennessee.

"We felt somewhat disappointed," he wrote regarding being left behind by these two men, "but knowing that God is ever willing and able to help those that trust in him, we cast our fears on him, and went to work."

He kept the group of Cumberland County believers alive the best he could, not being an ordained minister, and saw response as the year 1877 started. Later on that year, Soule wrote about him as being active in the Mt. Gilead church. The next year, he reported on a follow-up visit to the church Soule had started near Pikeville, Tennessee.

"They move very slowly and need more of the grace of God to help them overcome," he wrote.

A Methodist minister in Grassy Cove tried to discredit him, but he pressed on. "I know what it is to be shut out of meeting-houses and to be forsaken by parents, brothers, sisters and friends for the truth's sake; but

I take it all to the Lord in prayer," he wrote. "Brethren, pray for the precious truth here, and for me."

The next year he wrote again about the struggling Mount Gilead church and was still working with them in 1888. He wrote of a Baptist meeting in Laurel Church "where Elder O. Soule delivered a course of lectures about 12 years ago, meeting with strong opposition." J.M. Rees, the conference president, conducted some meetings there again, hoping to have sown some good seed.

Patrick Moyers died at his home in Graysville, Tennessee in 1910. "Brother Moyers was one of the first Adventists in the state of Tennessee and for several years was a licensed minister in the Seventh-day Adventist denomination," his obituary stated.

Samuel Fulton

At the 1881 General Conference session in Battle Creek the entire denomination mourned the death of Adventist pioneer leader James White. It was at this meeting that the Committee on Destitute Fields recommended that a young Minnesota minister transfer to Tennessee. Samuel Fulton accepted this call and was so effective that persecution set in, especially among his West Tennessee converts. The resulting court trials brought the Adventist movement into the national news media.

Fulton started out working with Squire Osborn in The Ridge Church, Goodlettsville, the Cumberland Mountains and Springville. He then went on his own to revive the Cross Plains Church, baptizing three people. He had less success in Pleasant View, across the line in Cheatham County but found a good audience near Clarksville in Henrietta and Woodford.

Back in Springville, he started meetings two miles out of town, and then moved on to Huntingdon, accompanied by the William Dortches of Springville. His meetings resulted in six people keeping the Sabbath there despite opposition from the local ministers.

At Leach, Tennessee, in the summer of 1883, he conducted meetings by invitation, and 32 people agreed to keep the Sabbath.

"The interest at this place is on the increase," Fulton and Dortch reported from Leach. "Many honest souls are gladly receiving the truth, and we have reason to believe that the Lord is influencing the minds of the people to accept his truth. We also know that Satan is not sleeping; his emissaries are at work. A letter has been found at the tent, threatening that if we do not leave within a specified time, we shall be driven out of the (Carroll) county.

"We have been here about seven weeks. Eighty-four are keeping the Sabbath, the majority of which are grown persons and heads of families. Our expenses thus far have been quite fully met. The people receive us gladly at their homes, and a great research is being made in the Scriptures to know whether these things are so."

That kind of success generated a backlash, as his next report in the *Review* indicated. "Since our last report, the enemies to the cause of truth have burned our tent," reported Fulton and Dortch. "We never experienced more fierce opposition than is manifested by the different denominations. The shattered factions of the different churches are uniting their forces, which have for years been bitterly opposed to each other, for the purpose of exterminating the truth, if possible. Three opposition sermons have been delivered against the Sabbath, but the effort was abortive, and now quite a sum of money is offered to one of the champions of the State to come to the rescue. He is expected next week. The work of the enemy has seemed thus far to increase the interest and more fully develop those who have accepted the truth."

Fulton pressed on. "The sum of $140 has been subscribed to purchase another tent; a meeting house is also in process of erection, which will be ready for service in less than two weeks. Our courage in the Lord is good as we see his work advancing in the earth."

With a new church under construction and 60 people joining the Sabbath School in Leach, the conference officials decided to hold the 1883 camp meeting there.

"This is where the truth has met with such determined opposition," wrote A.O. Burrill and M.B. Miller in reporting on it. "We went to the very spot where the tent was burned, and where Brother Fulton stood by a large tree and spoke to the 100 who came with a volunteer guard of 12 more men armed with loaded muskets."

Someone had circulated a notice reading, "We wish the people of Carroll County to understand that if they allow any more preaching from the Adventists in any of their houses or meeting-houses or school-houses, we will positively burn them up, if fire will burn them; and if he don't take his crowd and leave the country we will cut his head off and steak it at the forkes of the road. We mean what we say."

That threat rallied Fulton's followers, some willing even to defend him with their guns if necessary. They built a church and bought a big camp meeting tent. "We doubt if there would now be a church building there had it not been for the burning of the tent," the report said. "This was one of the times when the wrath of Satan is made to praise God."

The baptisms in Leach continued; the session elected Fulton president of the conference and Tract and Missionary Society; a church of 30 members was organized; and steps were taken to start a school in the new church building.

Samuel Fulton and J.H. Dortch next reported holding meetings in Callicott's Mills, Tennessee, in May of 1884, leaving behind there six people keeping the Sabbath, and went on to Martin in Weakley County. Two Dortch brothers from Springville worked with Fulton here, with William helping with evangelistic meetings and John Dortch canvassing in the Martin area.

The 1884 Tennessee Conference session, presided over by Samuel Fulton, admitted the Leach church into its corporate membership, bringing the total number of congregations to five.

Fulton began 1885 by visiting isolated Sabbath keepers and his main churches— Springville, Leach, Cross Plains and Nashville. He reported that the Springville people busied themselves by making tents for the next camp meeting: small tents to stay in and a large tent for the meetings.

He then reported bitter opposition to the work of Brethren Sisley and Rogers in the Sumner County hamlet of Mitchellville, but 12 people keeping the Sabbath. "We hope to organize a church in the near future." Later in 1885, the conference accepted a church in nearby Corinth into its fellowship.

Work there got off to a fast start. "He said that at Corinth, opposition ministers criticizing his work resulted in "several additions to the truth." He reported a Sabbath School membership there of 30.

At Mitchellville, ten miles from Corinth, Fulton said the meetings there had gone on for five weeks and created quite a stir in this remote spot in Tennessee, near the Kentucky state line. Some from Franklin had crossed the border to attend the meetings.

Fulton's work was not all evangelism. He felt the political pressure from people opposed to the seventh-day Sabbath. "A private letter from Elder Fulton, very recently received, states that the pressure is already becoming very heavy, and that it threatens to greatly impede our work," reported George I. Butler in the Feb. 9, 1886, *Review*. "Many arrests are being made, and he sees no escape for the arrested parties, but expects many of them will have to lie in jail."

The next week, Fulton wrote that "the justice of the peace made a mistake in issuing the warrants, which their lawyer was not slow to take advantage of, and the cases were consequently thrown out. Of course the relief thus obtained is only temporary, unless the Lord shall interpose to turn the counsel of Ahithophel into foolishness every time."

Despite the opposition, evangelical work continued to advance. By mid-1886, Fulton reported the experimental work of selling Adventist books in West Tennessee had been a great success, with 700 copies of *Marvel of Nations* being sold. The Leach Church enjoyed another successful series of meetings and boasted a Sabbath School membership approaching 70. Fulton also started meetings in Big Sandy and Trezevant.

The 1886 camp meeting was held in Paris, the location of the jail housing several believers convicted of working on Sunday.

"On the Sabbath, we visited the jail and had a short prayer-meeting with our brethren in bonds," wrote Fulton. "While we sang and prayed with them, the Lord seemed to come very near by his Spirit."

The 1886 session of the Tennessee Conference relieved Samuel Fulton of his presidential duties, and he continued in charge of the colporteur work. According to his *Review* obituary, health problems forced him to leave Tennessee for Florida and then the Pacific Northwest, where he died in 1890 at the age of 42.

Charles M. Kinney

Black members comprised part of the first Edgefield Junction congregation in Tennessee and were an active part of the conference from then on.

The first recorded black Adventist minister in Kentucky and Tennessee, a middle-aged man transferring from the West named Charles M. Kinney, traveled to Louisville to preach the Advent message in 1889.

He was born into slavery in Richmond, Virginia in 1855 and moved west "after the emancipation" according to his obituary in the *Review*. He attended

Charles M. Kinney, the first ordained black minister to work in Kentucky and Tennessee.

a series of evangelistic meetings conducted by J.N. Loughborough and Ellen White in Reno, Nevada, and joined the church there, rising to the office of secretary of their tract society. He attended Healdsburg College in California for two years, and then trekked to Kansas to sell Adventist literature. In 1889, the year of his ordination to the Adventist ministry, Pastor Kinney moved to Louisville.

He reported an active distribution of literature there, organized a church, and baptized nine new members.

"They have begun to pay tithes," Kinney wrote. "Some have realized a cross in this, but they purposed to be faithful, and thus not be found breaking the eighth commandment while trying to keep the fourth."

He described his Louisville church as "the second colored SDA Church in the world, so far as I know," the Edgefield Junction Church, organized about seven years previous, being the first. This group had had little ministerial help, and only about three sermons had been preached to them during the whole of their existence as far as he could tell; nevertheless they responded to him and promised to do their best.

He next reported on an 1890 camp meeting held in Guthrie, Kentucky. "I preached to my people once there, and once in a schoolhouse about a mile and a half from the campground, the next day after the meeting closed," he wrote. "I learned in passing through Guthrie (a few weeks later) that as the result of the two camp meetings there, several of my people are trying to keep the Sabbath."

He also preached four sermons at Harts Hill, a small black settlement just outside of Gallatin, Tennessee. Kinney then contacted isolated believers in Davidson and Cheatham Counties, in Nebo, Kentucky, and then in Fulton, Kentucky, as well as in Bowling Green, organizing a church there with eight members in 1891.

Kinney started a Sabbath School of eight members in Nashville in 1893 and hoped that would ripen into a church, doing much house-to-house work as well as preaching every Sunday night.

"We have been branded as 'liars' and 'false prophets' and the people warned not to allow us to come into their houses; but we believe the Lord will cause the wrath of man to praise him, and the remainder of wrath God will restrain," he wrote. "So we are laboring on in courage and hope.

"Our work in Nashville thus far has had some interruptions, and is therefore moving slowly, contending with opposition from the ministers, etc.; but with perseverance and the blessings of God more fruit will soon appear," he wrote in 1894. "We ask the prayers of all who are interested in work among the colored people."

His wife becoming an invalid forced Pastor Kinney to retire from active ministerial labor in 1911, and he moved into a room at the Riverside Hospital in Nashville after her death 26 years later. He lived there to the ripe old age of 96, dying in 1951.

William Covert

In 1888, an Indiana minister named William Covert, the first president of that conference, took charge of Adventist work in Tennessee and would make enough impact to attract violence, at least in one small West Tennessee town.

His first official notice in the Dec. 4, 1888, *Review* called for a general get-acquainted meeting in Springville. The fact that members were then still scattered is evidenced in his next notice, which asked them to send their tithes to the conference treasurer at Cross Plains if they did not give through a local church.

He next wrote a good report of three regional meetings held at Springville, Leach and Cross Plains, noting that Adventism was starting to mature.

"This church (Cross Plains) has been organized about ten years; thus all the novelty of hearing an Adventist has worn away and considerable prejudice exists. Nevertheless, many who have been opposed came to our meetings, and persuaded their neighbors to do so."

He reported two or three families accepting the Adventist message in Jackson, as well as a substantial sale of Adventist books to people who had attended his meetings there.

Then on June 28, 1889, he opened meetings in the Dyer County community of Lane and reported that "the opposition is the most bitter and satanic that I have ever met during the fourteen years that I have labored in the cause.

"One arrest has been made for Sunday work, and doubtless others will be made," he continued. "The opposition is not content with prosecution, but they have organized a religious Kuklux mob, who use shot-guns and revolvers instead of scriptural argument. A mob of this character raided us last night while I was preaching. They fired fifteen or twenty shots, with evident design to kill. One shot was fired at a brother who sat in a window. They evidently tried to shoot another brother, who is being prosecuted

Elder Kinney preached to a Methodist congregation in this church building near Gallatin, Tennessee, in 1890. A Baptist group still worships in this same sanctuary.

Other Early workers

LEACH SEVENTH-DAY ADVENTIST CHURCH

IN OCT 1883 SAMUEL FULTON, PRESIDENT OF THE TENNESSEE CONFERENCE OF SEVENTH-DAY ADVENTISTS, HELD A TENT MEETING AT 955 GRIGGS CHAPEL ROAD. HIS SONGLEADER BILLY DORTCH, AND THEIR WIVES ASSISTED ELDER FULTON. AFTER EVERYONE HAD LEFT THE MEETING, SOMEONE BURNED THE TENT AN TACKED A NOTE TO A NEARBY WHITE OAK TREE. THE NOTE STATED, "IF FULTON PREACHES ANYMORE WE WILL CUT OFF HIS HEAD AND PUT IT ON A STAKE AT THE OF THE ROAD." NINE-YEAR OLD JOHNNY KELLY FOUND THE NOTE AND BROUGHT IT TO THE CONGREGATION ON SABBATH MORNING. FULTON ASKED IF HE SHOULD CONTINUE TO PREACH, AND IT WAS AGREED HE SHOULD CONTINUE. SEVENTEEN-YEAR ANDERSON LEWIS ALONG WITH JOHN IKE REEVES AND SOME OTHER MEN STOOD GUAR WITH SHOTGUNS WHILE FULTON PREACHED.

PEOPLE GAVE OFFERINGS FOR A NEW TENT AND TO BUILD A CHURCH. TREES FRO JOHNNY LEACH'S PROPERTY WERE FELLED AND A NEW LOG CHURCH WAS BUILT AT 780 GRIGGS CHAPEL ROAD.

THE FIRST CONGREGATION INCLUDED ABOUT 30 MEMBERS. CHARTER MEMBERS INCLUDED JOHN AND SARAH LEACH AND THEIR DAUGHTER, SOPHIA; SAM AND MARTHA ESKEW; NATHANIEL PEARSON; MR AND MRS GEORGE COOK; ANDERSON LEWIS, HIS MOTHER JANE LEWIS KELLY AND HIS SISTER MAGGIE LEWIS WILLIAMS; AND ANNIE HAYNES. EARLY PIONEERS FOR THE WORK OF THE CHURCH INCLUDED T W KIVETT, WILLIAM KEELE, AND ROSCOE BURR. ELDER BURR, BORN IN THE CEDAR GROVE AREA, LATER BECAME PRESIDENT OF THE TENNESSEE RIVER CONFERENCE OF SEVENTH-DAY ADVENTISTS AND CONTRIBUTED TO THE GROWTH OF THE WORK OF THE CHURCH IN HIS HOME COMMUNITY.

THE CHARTER MEMBERS BELIEVED A CHRISTIAN EDUCATION WAS IMPORTANT AND STARTED THE FIRST CHURCH SCHOOL IN 1884. MRS SAMUEL FULTON SERVED AS THE FIRST TEACHER AND CONDUCTED CLASSES IN THE LITTLE LOG CHURCH.

THE CONGREGATION MET IN THE LOG CHURCH UNTIL 1910, WHEN BROTHER CARTER LED AN EFFORT TO BUILD A SMALL FRAME CHURCH WHERE THE PRESENT CHURCH IS LOCATED ON HIGHWAY 70. IN 1943 MEMBERS, LED BY ELDER VICTOR ESQUILLA, REPLACED THE FRAME CHURCH WITH A BRICK VENEER CHURCH. IN 1970 ELDER GORDAN COLLIER WITH THE HELP OF THE CHURCH BOARD LED A BUILDING PROJECT TO BUILD THE PRESENT CHURCH.

MARKER ERECTED SEPT 27 2003

This marker tells the story of the threats against Elder Samuel Fulton when he held his initial evangelistic meetings in Leach, Tennesse.

for Sunday work. They also shot through the wall of the frame building in such a way as to cause the ball to pass through the space where I had been standing behind the desk; but I had just stepped from behind it when the bullet crashed through the wall. They shot through the wall of the building, and, it is claimed, some shots came through the window when there were about 60 persons in the room; but providentially no one was hit."

This violence backfired on the perpetrators. "This course has made friends for us, and we hope for the cause of truth also," Covert wrote. "Many offer to come and guard the house nights during preaching services. It has been thought advisable to hold our services during the daytime, when the mob will not come. Perhaps we shall choose the latter, as it may not be best to raise a religious war just now. The plan of attack was made before I came. They do not want me present when Brother King is tried before the magistrate for working on Sunday."

Elder Covert went on to be president of the Vermont, Wisconsin, and Northern Illinois conferences, according to his obituary in the *Review*, and died in 1917 at the age of 75.

Ray Kelly of the Leach SDA Church stands where local opponents threatened to hang the head of an Adventist evangelist.

Samuel Fulton and William Dortch pitched a tent near these flags in Leach, Tennessee. A mob burned the tent, and the Adventist converts responded by building a church and school.

These early workers labored without the advantages of salaries, budgets or titles. But despite no money, jobs or social status combined with great opposition, their work bore rich fruit. These difficult Adventist conditions produced some outstanding workers for the church in the years ahead, many of whom left a lasting mark.

Early Prominent Families

Becoming an Adventist always has involved more profound changes in lifestyle than most people are prepared to make, placing new converts out of step with the fine folks they have known all their lives.

Of course their new family becomes the church. But after the Civil War, no such fellowship of believers existed in Kentucky and Tennessee. The early excitement of a Bible truth discovery could fade quickly once the newness wore off and reality set in.

Nevertheless, though scattered from fellow believers and pressed with poverty, some people accepted Adventism wholly and grew mature in the faith.

In Tennessee, some of the early converts endured enough arrests and court trials to make national news, as well as mention in the columns of the *Review*. Other people they discipled later distinguished themselves in Adventist denominational service, exemplifying how persecution can be the best thing to happen to a church.

The following families were not the only ones to keep the faith under trying circumstances; they are simply some who became well-known, but they represent many courageous believers whose names we may not learn until eternity.

The Dortch Family

According to an early history of the Springville SDA Church, George and John Dortch had gone from Springville, Tennessee, to Texas in 1878 and heard Elder R.M. Kilgore preach the Adventist message. George Dortch accepted it, but John turned it down and went back home. The conviction wouldn't go away, and John finally accepted the Sabbath. Hearing of G. K. Owen, a Seventh-day Adventist minister in the state, he and his fellow Springville believers sent for him.

Early in 1879, Elder Owen traveled there to conduct evangelistic meetings in Henry County and reported 16 people signing the covenant, five of whom were already keeping the Sabbath when he first arrived. The entire Dortch family accepted Adventism.

Elder Owen organized the Springville SDA Church on June 22, 1879, with six charter members: J.H. Dortch, William Dortch, Mrs. William Dortch, Mrs. Clark Dortch, Mrs. Mattie Fuich Moyers, and W.D. Dortch.

Elder Owen reported a bitter opposition, with W.D. Dortch taken to court for practicing his newfound faith.

This family would be prominent in the 19th century Adventist church in Tennessee. Owen reported ordaining W.D. Dortch as a local elder later that year in his *Review and Herald* account of the Tennessee Conference quarterly meeting.

Brother Dortch then helped Elder Samuel Fulton conduct meetings in Huntingdon, going on to even more fruitful meetings in the Carroll County community of Leach. Opponents burned their evangelistic tent there in the summer of 1883. The two workers responded by building a church.

Both W.D. and J.H. Dortch were active in the Tennessee Tract Society, which sold and distributed Adventist literature. J.H. Dortch wrote a brief note in the January 2, 1883 *Review* about his encounter with a hostile Baptist minister.

"Brother Fulton gave a course of lectures at a place about two miles north of Springville," he wrote. "Soon after he was gone, a Baptist minister came and tried to tear down the truth by preaching that the law is abolished, claiming that it was an impossibility to keep the Sabbath. I have just reviewed him before a good congregation. I had freedom in speaking, and think if ever strength was brought out of weakness, it was on this occasion. The people listened attentively, and some were affected to tears. I cannot tell what the result may be, but hope the seed of truth sown may be as bread cast upon the waters, that shall be gathered after many days."

J.H. Dortch then proceeded to Callicott's Mills, conducting meetings and selling books with Samuel Fulton.

The fifth annual session of the Tennessee Conference, held at the soon to become a university town of Martin listed J.H. Dortch on the nominations committee, his brother

G.W. Dortch on the Conference Committee, and W.D. Dortch on the Camp Meeting Committee.

In 1886, G.W. Dortch reported conducting a six-week series of meetings in Big Sandy, with the Methodist minister publicly opposing the Sabbath question.

"He took the position that the law is unchangeable; but as the commandment does not say the seventh day *of the* week, we have a perfect right to rest upon any day we choose, after working six days," he and Samuel Fulton wrote. "But as the laws of the land have determined the first day as the Christian Sabbath, we should observe that day."

Eight adults started keeping the Sabbath there and planned to join the Springville Church, 50 miles from Martin. Fulton and Dortch next traveled on to Trezevant.

W.D. Dortch pledged to sell Adventist books at camp meeting and had delivered 126 copies of the book *Marvel of Nations* by November of 1886. He reported that all West Tennessee canvassers combined had sold about 1,500 copies of this book during the year.

By the following November of 1887, J.H. Dortch was secretary of the Tennessee Tract Society, according to its report in the *Review*.

At the 1889 Tennessee Conference meeting, J.H. Dortch served on the Auditing Committee, G.W. Dortch on the Nominations Committee, and W.D. Dortch on the Licenses and Credentials Committee.

After the Tennessee Conference became the Tennessee River Conference in 1889,

W.D. Dortch served on the Auditing Committee and J.H. Dortch was listed as secretary of the conference and appointed to the Conference Committee according to the *Review*.

In the May 4, 1891, *Review,* W.D. Dortch reported organizing his people to canvass in Nashville, Tennessee and build up the church there. "We have a good Sabbath School here (numbering sixteen), for which we feel very thankful," he wrote. "Our school is held at the home of Sister Jenkins, who long has stood alone here in this city, and battled for the truth. We hope she will be rewarded in the kingdom of God for her kindness to us since we came here."

The next year, W.D. Dortch of Springville served on the 1892 Camp Meeting Committee to plan for services in Nashville, Tennessee.

According to his obituary, W.D. Dortch became an Adventist in 1878 and died in 1939 at the age of 81.

The *Review* obituary of his brother, George W. Dortch, said he was born in Henry County, Tennessee on April 3, 1851, became an Adventist in Texas as a young man, and then connected with the Battle Creek Sanitarium in 1890. He soon after started working with the *Review and Herald* there until moving back to Tennessee in 1907 to affiliate with the Southern Publishing Association. He died in Nashville in 1923.

In an 1889 *Review* obituary a Middia Dortch was listed as dying in Springville. She was the wife of William Dortch, aged 60 years (presumably one of the older men arrested and jailed for working on Sunday). Her obit added she had become an Adventist at the meetings conducted in Springville by G.K. Owen.

The Lowry Family

William Sidney Lowry, born March 28, 1862, in Springville, Tennessee, accepted the Adventist message in 1885 and became a minister, according to his obituary in the *Review*. He and his wife had two sons born to them about the time they joined the church, Gentry (b. 1884) and Charles (b. 1886), both of whom grew up to become prominent missionaries to Southern Asia.

According to early church records, the Lowry family joined the Lane SDA Church in 1891. Both their boys were baptized there.

Charles Lowry attended college at Graysville, Tennessee; Keene, Texas; and Washington Missionary College. He served as pastor in Jackson, Tennessee; Paducah, Kentucky; and Memphis Tennessee. He was ordained to the ministry at the 1915 camp meeting in Hazel, Kentucky, and went to Burma as a mission superintendent in 1916.

"Setting to work at once to learn the Burmese language, he made steady progress in spite of many responsibilities, and was soon preaching in the native tongue," stated his obituary in the May 22, 1919, *Review*. "Brother Lowry was a man of faith and prayer, and believed this message fully. His whole heart was in Burma. The people and their great need appealed to him very strongly. He willingly took the risks incidental to mission labor in the tropics, and paid the full price. While visiting the mission stations in company with Brethren Andross, Flaiz and Fletcher, he was taken ill and was brought back to his home in Rangoon. His disease

Gentry Lowry was a prominent missionary to India.

was pronounced smallpox, and resulted fatally after a struggle of about ten days. His death is a heavy blow to the work in Burma."

Charles' brother Gentry attended Hazel Academy in Kentucky and studied for the ministry at Southern Training School, Graysville, Tennessee, graduating in 1908. He worked in Tennessee, Kentucky, and Mississippi, being ordained in the latter state in 1909. That same year, he and his wife accepted a call to India. After learning the Tamil language, he served as teacher and evangelist, and as principal of the South India Training School, now Spicer Memorial College. He later went on to become superintendent of two unions in India and then, in 1941, president of the Southern Asia Division.

"He organized the first Sabbath School in South India, and wrote the first Bible lessons used in our schools in that field," according to a tribute to him in the July 30, 1942, *Review and Herald*. "He has written books and tracts and innumerable articles descriptive of life and work in India and expositive of present truth. As teacher, preacher, organizer, author, and executive, he has given a distinctive mold for more than three decades to our work in the Southern Asia Division."

Gentry Lowry (right) died on May 4, 1942, in Western India, after Burma had just fallen to the Japanese during those desperate early days of World War II.

His wife Bertha, daughter of an early Tennessee conference worker, stayed on in India until her death in 1975. Roscoe Lowry, son of Bertha and Gentry Lowry, kept the family tradition alive by also serving as president of the Southern Asia Division.

The Yates Family

In 1878, Squire Osborn held meetings in Cross Plains, Tennessee. The next year, Clifton Owens wrote in the *Review* that he had held a good Sabbath meeting there in the home of Brother Yates.

"The next day we assembled a mile and a half from town, and organized a Sabbath School of nine members, expecting that more will be added soon," Owens wrote. "There is a company of ten Sabbath keepers here, who should very soon be organized. The interest is good."

The Yates name appeared prominently in conference meetings and church activities after that, showing Cross Plains to be a center of early Adventism, with the Yates family in a leadership role.

G.K. Owen organized the Cross Plains Church in July of 1879, ordaining Brother Yates as an elder. At the formation of the Tennessee Conference on October 7, 1879, the delegates chose J.B. Yates to serve on the first executive committee and elected him a temporary president of the conference in 1881 until the next regular session, due to the departure of some officers. Another member of this important group was

J.E. White, also of Cross Plains. He may have been a businessman, because this conference also appointed him to serve on the committees on auditing and credentials. The regular conference session in October of that year elected Squire Osborn as president and J.B. Yates as part of the three-person Executive Committee. He also served as vice president of the Tennessee Sabbath School Association.

J.B. Yates and J.E. White continued to serve on important Tennessee Conference committees in 1884 and 1887. In 1889, the conference president asked all isolated members to send their tithes to J.B. Yates in Cross Plains.

This Cross Plains church died off for a few years, but the Yates family remained active there. Local records showed J.B. Yates as having many relatives. A John J. Yates, born in 1831 according to local genealogical records, was the father of John B. Yates as well as of a John Spain Yates (1888-1950),

Alvin Yates worked for years to revive the Cross Plains SDA Church.

whose obituary said he was born in Cross Plains, Tennessee of Adventist parents. He served as a conference worker and missionary to the Far East for many years. Serving five years in Java, he was "eminently successful in turning Mohammedans to Christianity," his obituary states. A Sowell Jefferson Yates became the father of Ola Yates Covert, (1872-1932, according to her obituary in the Southern Tidings) and Alvin Yates (1891-1976), a prominent Cross Plains businessman for many years [shown above]. He worked hard to revive the Cross Plains Adventist church, finally succeeding in 1958. Joseph E. White's daughter Ella married

A.A. McClanahan and was an active in the Nashville area for many years.

This rebuilt and remodeled church occupies the original site of the Lane SDA Church. Another denomination currently worships here.

The Lane SDA Church celebrated its 50th anniversary on August 28, 1937. Members of the Bittick, Callicott, Etheridge, Hamilton, Jensen, King, Lawson, McCullough, Roddy, Thurmon, Underwood, Wade and Walker families posed for this picture.

Other Early Families of Significance

The Lane, Tennessee SDA Church, founded amid violence, produced several other productive families besides the Lowrys, showing how persecution can be good news for a religious movement.

For instance, the Callicott family contributed several prominent people to Adventism. A Dolf Callicott was a member of the 1889 Tennessee River Conference Committee on Auditing.

According to an early Lane Church history, when the members planned for a building in 1890, L.A. Callicott gave the land and J.H. Callicott donated the lumber. L.A. Callicott was tried in a Dyersburg, Tennessee, court that same year for working on Sunday, and the judge ordered the jury to render a not-guilty verdict. He was elected to serve on the Tennessee River Conference Committee the next year.

L.A. Callicott later lived in Hazel, Kentucky, had eight children, and moved to Mercedes, Texas shortly before he died in 1909.

One of his daughters, Beulah Callicott, a pioneer student at Hazel Academy, graduated from Southern Training School in Graysville in 1907. She served as a church school teacher and Sabbath School secretary in the Tennessee River Conference, then secretary-treasurer of the Mississippi Conference and Tract Society.

The Callicotts produced many other notable people. Eva Callicott married Charles Lowry in 1910 and went with him to Burma as a missionary. Lois Callicott served as a missionary to India as the wife of J.B. Carter. Louise Carter Lowry likewise served in Burma. She was a great-granddaughter of J.H. Callicott, donor of the lumber for the original Lane Church. A Rees Callicott journeyed to Central America as a missionary, and C.R. Callicott served as secretary-treasurer of the Mexican Union Mission. Two brothers of Eva Callicott Lowry, Rex and Oakley Callicott, became successful businessmen in the United States, with Rex Callicott at one time known as the richest Adventist in the world.

Other productive Lane families were the Wades and Roddys.

Something about hard times gave these isolated believers the strength and spiritual oxygen to grow mature in the faith. Serious opposition produced some kind of a reaction to inspire them to press on in the Three Angels Messages. What should have been disappointment turned into victory.

The Law Challenges the Sabbath

The April 20, 1886, *Review* ran an article listing Tennessee as one of 12 states or territories not granting any exception to the law requiring Sunday observance. Fourteen states did exempt seventh-day keepers from Sunday law mandates, with Kansas not requiring Saturday military or jury duty should that violate religious conviction.

With the early Sabbath-keepers either not knowing about or ignoring the Ellen White counsel to devote Sunday to missionary work, because missionary work, unlike plowing a field, was not illegal, the opponents of Adventism used this legal opening against them. Tennessee Adventists commanded lots of media attention during the early 1890s, even though it had one of the smallest Adventist populations in North America.

Sunday-law proponents across Tennessee sent numerous Adventists to jail during the 1890s and even temporarily shut down a church-operated school in Graysville.

Pressure on West Tennessee Believers

Review and Herald coverage of Tennessee persecution started with a trial in Springville on February 8, 1886. Since the Justice of the Peace failed to file the proper paperwork, the case was thrown out of court.

The June 22, 1886 *Review* reported that a Grand Jury had indicted W.H. Parker, James Stem, and William Dortch of Springville for a Sunday law violation and fined them $30. They chose to work off the fine in jail at 25 cents a day, meaning 80 days of incarceration. The only other detail the *Review* editor knew was that the Tennessee Supreme Court sustained this prosecution, as did the same court in Arkansas for a similar situation there.

The editors, remote from Tennessee, asked for more information, and W.H. Parker of Springville shared the following details of the case in response.

"I, with Brethren James Stem and William Dortch, was indicted before the grand jury at the May term of the court of 1885, and was tried at the September term following, and found guilty by the court. Or rather, my case was tried, and a verdict of guilty being rendered by the jury, the judge set the fine at $20 and all the cost. The attorney for the State agreed with our attorney that the other two cases should not be tried, but abide the decision of my case in the Supreme Court. The Supreme Court confirmed the decision of the lower court, which settled a fine of $20 and the cost on each of us.

"Brother William Dortch will have to pay his, as he has the property from which they can collect the money. Brother Stem and I have no more property than is exempt from the execution by the law of the State. The law of the State is that if a person who is convicted of a misdemeanor is not able to pay his fine in money, he shall pay it in jail at 25 cents per day.

"We have concluded here that it is not best to pay a fine in money except we have violated a righteous law, and that we could bear a more effectual testimony for the truth by lying in jail than by working for money to pay a fine.

"There will be nothing further done in the case until the fourth Monday in September next; then we will have to pay it off or go to jail.

"Wages here are low. A good farm hand can get $10 or $12 a month. I am a blacksmith and wages maker. I make from one to two dollars per day when I work at my trade. I shall be 36 years of age in July next. Brother Stem is about 55, and Brother Dortch is 60 or over."

Parker added that they were thinking of paying court costs but not the fine. They had had some help with attorney fees and were willing to appeal all the way to the U.S. Supreme Court if necessary.

The judge fined each of them $10 plus court costs, the total adding up to around $40. They were of good courage and chose to spend six months in the Henry County jail in Paris rather than pay the fine.

Valuable Advertising

The trial attracted a great deal of positive attention to the Advent message. Pastor Fulton was conducting a tent meeting near the Paris church and attracting a crowd of people with a deep interest in the Adventist message. The trial also directed the attention of the public to the Tennessee camp meeting held in Paris that year. R.A. Underwood wrote in the *Review* that many of the leading citizens of Paris attended some of the meetings to learn why Adventists kept the seventh day of the week.

Three ministers from the General Conference attended and visited the three men imprisoned for keeping the Ten Commandments along with other criminals convicted of breaking them. The jailer granted the men a furlough from prison on Sabbath from 9 a.m. to 5 p.m. so they could attend services.

The Tennessee and Arkansas trials inspired the General Conference Committee on Prosecutions to bring the Adventist side of the issue to the general public.

Wider Impact

The imprisonment of people religiously keeping the Sabbath but doing secular work on Sunday also generated newspaper comment across the country.

"It is said that an inoffensive old man of 65 years of age is lying on the stone floor of a county jail in Tennessee for the 'crime' of working on Sunday, having observed Saturday as a day of rest and worship," commented the *Sentinel* of Chicago. "It would be worth while to see the lawmakers of that godly State when they stand up for judgment in the next world. If they don't have to attend fire a thousand years for every day that old man is in jail I don't want to march in any processions over the 'golden pavements' nor play a harp on the 'grassy banks' of beautiful rivers."

"We confess that we did not know that such laws existed in those States (Tennessee and Arkansas)," commented a later edition of the *Sentinel* in response to a letter on the issue from one of their Kansas readers. "Much less could we have been made to believe that officials could be found in this whole country who would be bigoted, intolerant, cruel, and damnable enough to perpetrate such an outrage in the name of law.

"In closing, Mr. Smith says that 'as a matter of fact, we have neither religious nor social liberty;' and we guess he is right."

The conference president and two other Adventist representatives went to Capitol Hill but failed to persuade the state legislature to pass a law exempting Sabbath-keepers from Sunday law penalties.

J.M. Rees, the conference president, then ran into violent opposition to meetings he had been invited to conduct in the Scott County community of Jeffers, Tennessee. A rough group surprised him and two other people walking home from a meeting. "To our astonishment a crowd of men had secreted themselves behind the bushes along the mountain road, and began stoning us," Rees wrote in the *Review*. "When they could no longer reach us in this way, they opened fire on us with their revolvers, shooting at us ten times; but we all passed through unharmed, although some of the large stones passed near enough to fan my face, and I could hear the whiz of the bullets. I never felt the Lord so near and so precious to my soul as I did at that time."

Reports of a threat to blow up the meeting house reached Rees, but he continued to a slight crowd; then an opposing Baptist minister obtained a warrant for his arrest. A state senator whom Rees had met in Nashville a few days prior saved him from having to go to jail, and at the trial, the plaintiffs withdrew their charges.

"I went back to my work rejoicing, esteeming it a blessing to be persecuted for the truth's sake," wrote Rees. "I announced that there would be a meeting the next day, and a goodly number were present. At the close of the meeting, twelve adults signed the covenant, and two others promised to keep the Sabbath. Thus closed my first effort in Scott County, Tennessee."

More Trouble in West Tennessee

The pro Sunday-law sentiment continued. The January 22, 1889, edition of the *Review* printed a hostile announcement circulated in Dyer County, Tennessee, dated Dec. 10, 1888 and signed by several people stating "That we, the undersigned citizens of the Texas neighborhood and vicinity, being desirous of the welfare of our community, and that peace may prevail, and that the morale of our children may not be insulted and trampled upon by willful violations of the Sunday laws of our land, on this day pledge our honor that we will individually and collectively prosecute each and every violation of our State law that may come under our observation."

The Springville Adventists had found the Sabbath message in Texas.

William Covert reported in the *Review* that in the Dyer County community of Lane, after his meetings, "Nearly all the interested ones were so intimidated by the mob violence that they ceased to attend. Those who began to attend were visited in the night with guns, and after shooting around them they were threatened, and ordered not to attend the Adventist meeting any more."

A Dyer County court fined Robert King $2 plus costs for working on Sunday. The justice of the peace admitted that Brother King had been the only one in his 28 years of service convicted for working on Sunday, when many people whom he knew earned money on that day.

"He said he could only execute the law as a civil magistrate," Covert continued. "Thus it is plain that the Sunday law of Tennessee is only used as an inquisitorial machine for the religious persecution of those who keep the seventh day. All are allowed to work on Sunday, provided that they do not keep the Sabbath. It is having the effect to make the men blood-thirsty who are doing the prosecuting. They are like ravenous wolves when they have scented the blood of their victim."

Under the title "A Curiosity," the *Review* ran two accounts of this Lane incident appearing in the secular media, one in denial.

"After diligent inquiry, I have failed to find out anything concerning any trouble in Dyer County, in which any Seventh-day Adventists are connected, as mentioned in the St. Louis *Globe-Democrat* of July 17," commented a writer to the *Weekly American* published in Nashville, Tennessee. "The whole thing is a fabrication, nothing of the kind having ever happened in Dyer County. There was, however, a report current that some trouble existed in Obion County, in which the Seventh-day Adventists were connected, but that report is discredited, and no credence given to it whatever. It is believed to be simply a Mulhatto yarn. Our grand jury is now in session, and the attorney-general informs me that nothing of the kind has been called to either his or the grand jury's attention. In fact, nothing of the kind or character has ever been heard of here, or within the borders of Dyer County."

Another writer, trying to smooth over the matter, contradicted this testimony. "For the last few years the Seventh-day Adventists have been visiting 'Texas,' preaching and distributing tracts, etc., and in this way have succeeded in making quite a number of converts, principally among the illiterate and poorer class of people," this person wrote. "The more cultured part of the neighborhood bore with it for some time, hoping that it would not result in an open violation of the recognized laws of the State; but, alas this was not the case, for Sunday in 'Texas' was fast losing its dignity and solemnity, and was being debauched and usurped into a common day for labor and general farm work. Alarmed at this state of things, some of Obion's best and most worthy citizens entered into an agreement to prosecute any person found violating or desecrating the Sabbath. . . Mr. R.M. King was arrested, and tried before Justice Barker for plowing on Sunday. King was fined three dollars and cost, which he refused to pay, saying he would plow again the next Sunday. King was released, and an execution was raised, and the fine and costs made out of his effects. He was also indicted at the last term of the circuit court at Troy, for the same offense. As for the shooting referred to in McKee's Inter Ocean article, your correspondent has it from a thoroughly reliable source that not a shot was fired with the intention of hitting any one."

"The foregoing shows that those who have had any connection with the disgraceful affair are evidently ashamed of themselves," commented the *Review*. "They are chagrined to have the public learn the facts in the case. But in attempting to discredit the reports that have gone all over the country, as must be the case from their being published in such large dailies as the Chicago *Inter Ocean* and the St. Louis *Globe-Democrat*, they have evidently failed to consult together; for the story of one destroys that of the other. The reports will doubtless still be credited."

Another news account reported the violence in this way: "Elder William Covert belongs to the Seventh-day Adventists, who believe in keeping Saturday holy instead of Sunday. He started some revival meetings in Tennessee, but in the midst of the preaching a mob rode up, armed with shot guns and revolvers, and fired fifteen or twenty rounds of shot into the Adventist building. They aimed directly at the Elder and several of the brethren, but fortunately the gunning was bad. Naturally, the meeting broke up in some haste. Then one man with orthodox shot-guns visited the homes of those who attended the meetings, and told them they would better keep away in future. They are bound to see that the Christian religion is respected in Tennessee."

Some Lane believers also went to trial for working on Sunday. Brethren Callicott and Stem appeared in the Dyersburg Circuit Court on November 25, 1889, under indictment for working on Sunday "to the great disturbance and common nuisance of the good citizens of their community." The jury found Callicott guilty but deadlocked regarding Stem. The judge thus ordered a new trial.

R.M. King went to trial in March, 1890, in the Obion County Circuit Court. His indictment charged him with "plowing on Sunday, (June 23, 1889) and doing various other kinds of work on that day and on Sundays before that day, without regard to said Sabbath days. Said work was not necessary, nor done as a matter of charity; and the doing of said work on said day was and is a disturbance to the community in which done, was offensive to the moral sense of the public, and was and is a common nuisance."

One witness testified he had seen Mr. King plowing his field on Sunday. The jury found him guilty after a half hour deliberation and fined King $75. He appealed to the Tennessee Supreme Court.

"The results of this case prove more clearly than ever the danger of removing a single provision that our fathers wisely put in the Constitution to protect the rights of conscience, and to secure to all perfect Religious Liberty," wrote Dan T. Jones in his account of the trial in the *Review*. "And it is not enough to have these safeguards in the Constitution. The statute-books, also, must be kept clear of laws touching matters that are purely religious."

The National Religious Liberty Association then published a 16-page tract on this trial and encouraged all church members to distribute it.

The Tennessee Supreme Court upheld the King verdict. E.E. Marvin, president of the Tennessee River Conference, predicted that this precedent would result in the indictment and trial of more Springville church members and appealed for people and means to distribute these religious liberty tracts in Henry and Carroll Counties.

"Believing the *Review* to be anxiously scanned each week to learn how the battle goes in Tennessee, I will state that the recent demonstrations of hatred against us and our work have by no means discouraged our people," wrote Elder Marvin in the July 29, 1890 *Review*. "There are no new developments to report. The inquisitors seem to be waiting for something. They are doubtless beginning to learn that they have a larger job on their hands than they at first imagined." He added that Brother King was still free pending an appeal to the federal court in Memphis.

At a retrial of L.A. Callicott on July 21, 1890, the judge ordered the jury to render a not guilty verdict. "Thus another State disgrace was rolled back upon the individuals who originated it," wrote E.E. Marvin. "We thank God for this victory for his dear cause."

The petition of R.M. King to the Memphis federal judge for a writ of habeas corpus drew a comment in the St. Louis *Globe Democrat*, describing it as "a case of national interest and importance."

"The case of Mr. King is to be made a test case, and no matter what the decision of Judge Hammond may be, an appeal will be taken to the Supreme Court of the United States," the newspaper commented. "The society of the Seventh-day Adventists does not recognize the Christian Sabbath, but observe Saturday as a day of rest, and insist upon working or seeking amusement, as they may see fit, upon the Christian Sabbath. The society contends that its members have a right to worship as they may choose, and observe such Sabbath day as they like; that under the Constitution of the United States they should be protected in their religious views. The case will be watched with interest, not only by this society, but by other sects who do not believe in the compulsory observance of the Christian Sabbath."

The trial began in Memphis early in 1891, recounting the circumstances of the case and the defense attorney presenting an able argument for religious liberty. The judge reserved his decision.

In the meantime, the *Review* ran comments from other publications around the country with opinions regarding the Tennessee persecutions.

"An exchange says, that in parts of Tennessee and other States, people are quite frequently imprisoned for working on the first day of the week, or Sunday, and people, too, who keep the seventh day as their Sabbath," said the Fontanelle (Iowa) *Observer*. "A law which would imprison a seventh-day (worshiper) is not right. It is interference where the law has no business—in the religious dictates of a man's conscience. We believe the first day is the proper day to observe, but if others wish to keep the seventh, they should have the same right to so do which we have to keep the first, and they should be protected in such right by law."

The *Christian Advocate* of Nashville, Tennessee, pointed out some inconsistencies in the Sunday laws. "The State of Tennessee has some very stringent Sunday laws," the paper commented. "Under these laws a number of Adventists, who observe the seventh day as a period of rest, have been subjected to indictment, trial, and penalty for working in their fields on the first day of the week. . . The civil law cannot, of course, constrain any man's conscience; but it may, without being charged with tyranny or oppression, require small minorities of the citizens of the commonwealth to avoid any outward acts offensive to the feelings and rights of the great majority."

That opinion summed up the opposition to the West Tennessee Adventists, but then this religious periodical pointed out a glaring contradiction.

"But the thing that puzzles us is this: Why should a few obscure farmers who are conscientious in refusing to comply with the demands of the general sentiment, be dealt with so severely, when great corporations are allowed the utmost liberty? Our railroads not only run the regular mail trains on the Lord's day, but they also send out the freight trains just as on any other day of the week, thus imposing upon the consciences of their employees, many of whom are Christian men, a very heavy burden. Why this inequality?

. . . If the rural communities of the State are to be protected against the scandal of a little plowing on the Lord's Day, why should not the whole State be protected against Sunday freight trains? There is a great army of sturdy and honest workmen, whose dependent families force them to stick to their tasks, but who would give no small sum if they could get a weekly rest."

King himself wrote a brief description of his predicament in the May 26, 1891, *Review*. He said he and his wife had started keeping the seventh day as Sabbath in 1884. Opposition had seemed to advertise the Sabbath, so the ministers had organized the people to enforce Sunday laws. He said four State Warrants had been served on him. The jailer had treated him well, not only allowing him to come and go from the prison, but even to attend weeknight religious services in a nearby Methodist Church.

Then the verdict finally came in mid-1891: Judge E.S. Hammond of the United States District Court in Memphis, Tennessee upheld the state courts. He reasoned that his court had no right to interfere in state common law. "The courts cannot in cases like this, ignore the existing customs and laws of the masses, nor their prejudices and passions even, to lift the individual out of the restraints surrounding him because of those customs and laws, before the time has come when public opinion shall free all men in the manner desired." Violation of law must be punished, and keeping the Sunday was law. "If man has set it apart in due form by his law for rest, it must be obeyed as man's law if not as God's law."

Brother King returned to jail pending an appeal to the U.S. Supreme Court. The *Review* published comments from several newspapers across the country. "As what has been in Tennessee accomplished against the Seventh-day people, may in other States beg against those of other beliefs, or no beliefs, it is important that each and all be on the alert for liberty," wrote the Hastings, Michigan, *Plaindealer* in describing the penalty as "outrageous."

"A local contemporary thinks that Tennesseans have a right to wreak religious bigotry on minorities in this fashion, and that if the members of the minority do not like it they can do as the Jews are doing in Russia—give up their homes and leave," commented the San Francisco *Examiner*. "This is not the common idea of American liberty. The principle at the root of our Government is that every man has a right to do as he pleases so long as he does not infringe the rights of anybody else. The attempt to confine a Seventh-day Adventist to five days' work a week when other people are allowed to work six, is a discrimination so unjust that it ought to make a Tennessean ashamed to acknowledge his State.

"Californians have much to be thankful for, but nothing more than that they live in a community in which people mind their own business, each disposing of his time as he sees fit, and allowing his neighbors to do the same."

The New York *Independent* conceded that the decision of a federal judge not to review a case of a conviction under process in State law may have been legally correct, but described the decision not to allow a man to work on Sunday after resting on Saturday—without interfering with the rest of others—as "bad law, and bad morals, and bad religion."

The editor of *Arena*, a national magazine, regarded the decision as a dangerous form of conservatism seeking to legally "fetter thought, crush liberty, and throttle the vanguard of progress." He compared Mr. King's status as an outsider to that of the 12 disciples of Jesus Christ in Roman society. He feared the law was passing into the hands of "small men and narrow minds" paying little heed to the guarantees of the Constitution.

"Comparatively few of the leading secular journals have deemed this outrage sufficiently important to call for editorial comment, notwithstanding it marks the establishment of a precedent which must inevitably work great misery to innocent people at the hands of religious fanatics, unless there is a sufficient agitation to cause the repeal of many iniquitous laws which are a menace to the rightful freedom of citizens as long as they remain on the statute books," the editor concluded.

The King case stayed in the news throughout 1891. "The attention being attracted by the case of Brother King becomes more remarkable every week," commented the November 24, 1891 *Review*. "The papers in all sections of the country are commenting upon it, and very much is being done in this way to call attention to the truth by circulating knowledge of our people and work." The *Review* then ran an editorial from the prestigious *Central Law Journal* citing the importance of the case.

But before the Supreme Court could rule, Brother King died and precipitated more Springville arrests that had been put on hold. A Brother J. Moon shared the details with A.O. Tait of the General Conference Religious Liberty Department in a letter published in the April 26, 1892 *Review*. "One of our neighbors was at the county seat on business, and the State's attorney came in and asked him if he lived in the Advent community," Moon wrote. "He replied that he did. The attorney asked, 'Do they keep up their Sunday work?' He answered, 'Yes, and none of the Adventists will deny it.'

"Then the attorney requested him to give him the names of five of the leading church members, which he did. The State's attorney said he had heard the circuit judge, Judge Swiggart, say he was going to put a stop to that Sunday desecration.

"So the five warrants were issued, and are in the sheriff's hands. But it seems that he has understood that we will not give bonds, and so will wait until court sits which will be the fourth Monday in May."

W.E. Colcord and J.E. Rogers of the General Conference in Battle Creek attended the trial in Paris, along with a Chicago Baptist minister named G.W. Ballenger. All five defendants represented themselves in court and were tried separately.

The judge declared one man innocent and mitigated the sentences of the others, since they would not pay the $25 fine but chose to work it off in jail at a credit of 25 cents per day. The cost to the county of each man's serving 100 days, or a total of 400 days for the four of them, would be considerable, and both the judge and jailer felt it would be in the best community interest not to spend all this money. The judge therefore decided to fine them just $1 and costs, threatening a heavier fine next time.

"The attorney general says the work must stop, and the judge said the same in a very pleasant way," wrote W.A. Colcord in the *Review*. "While attending the trials, we learned that the grand jury then in session was already getting out new indictments against our brethren for more recent Sunday work."

"Our brethren who have been prosecuted for Sunday labor in Tennessee are now lying in jail," wrote A.O. Tait, corresponding secretary of the National Religious Liberty Association, in the June 14, 1892 *Review*. "Their imprisonments came just at a time when they should be putting in their crops, and unless we help them, their families will have to suffer."

Readers responded with contributions, including fellow believers in College Place, Washington, who sent them $20 collected at a 4th of July church picnic.

Then J.H. Dortch reported that the court had ordered a seizure of his property in order to pay the fines, meaning he would be freed from jail.

"In this fact there is an important lesson for all our people," wrote A.O. Tait. "We have had warning after warning, for years, through the *Testimonies*, stating that our property would finally be seized to pay these fines wrongfully imposed upon us. Why not use all our surplus property now in the spread of the truth, before they have a chance to take it from us?"

This condemnation of his property must not have been carried out, for Brother Dortch wrote a letter from the Henry County jail thanking the *Review* readers for their support. The experience, he said, had strengthened their faith, and he told of the conversion of their Sabbath School superintendent dating to the time his father previously served time in jail for religious reasons.

"We will be here from forty-five to sixty-four days, from the time we came here," he wrote. "We are permitted to send and receive our mail, and we are allowed to get our drinking water, also to have a walk each day. We have many good books to read, and are all permitted to be together, each of us having a chair. We have cleaned the jail the best we could, and we are quite comfortable to what we were at the first. We want to tender our thanks to the many dear brethren and sisters for their good letters to us. Time passes away rapidly here. The good Lord blesses us every day. We praise his holy name."

After Dortch was released from prison, having spent the latter part of his sentence working on a chain gang with some of the local criminals, the district attorney summoned 18 of his neighbors before another Grand Jury, asking them if they had seen him working on Sunday.

"I guess he thinks he [the district attorney] will be as good as his word," Dortch wrote. "He told C.P. Bollman he was going to prosecute every man, woman, and child till this thing was stopped. O brother Tait, it is coming harder and harder, and our only hope is in God, and in him we can be free indeed and in truth."

The June 28, 1892 *Review* issue printing Dortch's letter from the Henry County Jail carried a story on the same page of arrests for Sunday labor in Graysville, Tennessee, site of a successful new Adventist school.

"It seems that the influence of our work is making a very favorable impression upon the citizens of that place, and when it came to be understood that a couple of our brethren were arrested for Sunday labor, the indignation of the whole community was aroused against it, and as a result, the case against our brethren was not permitted to come to trial; but an agreement was reached by which the case was dismissed from court," wrote A.O. Tait. "The State's attorney said that if the case had come to trial, he was very sure that our brethren would have been convicted."

These unjust Tennessee jailings also stimulated a greater religious liberty work by the General Conference. A.O. Tait wrote in the December 6, 1892, *Review* that after the editor of the influential *Boston Arena* read "In the Chain Gang," an account of the Tennessee Sunday law problems, he had written an editorial condemning this injustice and allowed the General Conference to reproduce it and send it out to media people across the country. The next issue of the *Review* called on all Adventists to sympathize with Methodists in Austria, who were having as hard a time with the governing authorities there as were the Tennessee believers with the authorities here.

The trials seemed to be good for the Springville Church. W.S. Lowry reported a successful week of prayer there. "I never witnessed such an outpouring of the Holy Spirit as we had during the whole time of the meetings."

He reported the completion of a new church building and told of five men leaving their work to sell Adventist literature. "Notwithstanding these persecutions that are brought to bear upon this church, I never saw it in any better condition spiritually than it is at the present time," he added.

Suddenly, when it had seemed that the law would do all in its power to shut down Adventism in Springville, the prosecution died down.

"We are just in receipt of a letter from Elder C.L. Boyd, stating that our brethren in Springville, Tenn., who were to have been tried last week for Sunday labor, have been released," wrote A.O. Tait in the June 13, 1893, *Review*. "The judge, with the consent of the jury, discharged both of the brethren without committing their cases to the jury. Brother Boyd further states that he was informed on good authority that the judge refuses to authorize the attorney general to prosecute any more of our people there in the name of the State, but requires that a prosecuting witness enter the complaint and appear as the prosecutor. This will shut off the persecutions and prosecutions of the attorney general, unless he can find some one like minded with himself, who would be willing to appear as prosecuting witness." Boyd added that some people were deliberately avoiding the Adventists on Sunday so they could not testify against them.

But people there still opposed the Sabbath. "Yet the spirit of persecution is not dead, by any means," Tait continued. "Some are offering themselves as prosecuting witnesses, and what may be the final outcome of the matter, we will have to wait to see."

But then the prosecutions shifted from Henry to Carroll County. "These arrests are coming thicker and faster all the time," wrote A.O. Tait. "And should we not see in them the clearest fulfillments of prophecy and the beginning of the great persecution to which we expect to be subjected a little later on? Now is our time for earnest labor."

The *Review* also reported arrests of Adventists in Maryland.

In the Weakley County town of Dresden, W.B. Capps was jailed because a neighbor saw him cutting corn stalks in his own field on a Sunday in May, 1892. Others saw him plowing and splitting rails on various Sundays, activities leading to his arrest on June 8, 1893. The court fined him $10 plus $41.80 in costs. The Tennessee Supreme Court affirmed the lower court, strapping Capps with fines and costs amounting to $110.45. Working this off in jail at 25 cents a day would take a year and nearly three months.

"Brother Capps has a wife 24 years of age, and four children, the eldest being only six years old, and one of them sick at the time of the father's imprisonment," wrote A.O. Tait in the July 10, 1894, Review. "His family is left all alone in the woods a quarter of a mile from any house. He is a poor man and unable to support his family during his confinement.

"This is one of the most severe sentences that has been inflicted on any of our brethren as yet, and it shows something of the spirit that is in the world, and what we may expect from now on until the end of time."

Two weeks later, R.G. Garrett wrote in the *Review* that he had responded to a request for ministerial labor in the Dresden area and found one of the grand jurors who had voted to indict Brother Capps now himself keeping the Sabbath along with his wife. "They said, 'We know it is right, and we have determined to obey;' wrote Garrett, "So we can say that the Lord makes the wrath of man to praise him."

"We hope, for the sake of Tennessee's reputation for intelligence and fair-mindedness, that the account may prove inaccurate," commented the Chicago *Herald*. "It is too late in the century for religious persecution of this sort."

The New Orleans *Times-Democrat* denounced the Capps imprisonment as "barbarous and unchristian" and started a fund to help bail him out of jail. The Plainfield, N.J., *Daily Press* did the same. Readers of the *American Hebrew* in New York bailed him out. The fine and court costs for Capps amounted to $72.25. He had served $24.25 of it in jail, and the Hebrews paid the rest, allowing Capps to go home after being held in prison for 97 days.

"A person reading about my case would naturally have thought that the Sunday advocates of Weakley County were very strict in executing the law on those who did not refrain from work on that day; but during my imprisonment, I saw the same kinds of work being done on Sunday that were followed every other day of the week," Capps wrote in the October 16, 1894, *Review*. "Beeves were killed and hauled through the town while I was in prison to the place of sale. Dry goods were sold, and bookkeeping was going on unmolested. The only ones that seemed to be called upon to suffer the penalty of the law were those who kept the Sabbath according to the commandment. By thus singling out and persecuting those who keep the commandments, it shows to unprejudiced minds that we are making progress toward the spirit of the Dark Ages. But thanks be to God who giveth us the victory through our Lord Jesus Christ."

"We are just informed by letter that Brother Plumb has been released from jail in Tennessee, several days before his time was out," wrote A.O. Tait in the November 27, 1894 *Review*. "While he was in jail, he acted as general chore boy for the jailer; went for the mail, attended to his cow, hauled fodder from five miles away, etc. Rather a strange criminal that could be trusted unguarded five miles from the jail. Criminals have been heard of that would not only have run away under such circumstances, but would have taken the team as well."

Attention Shifts Eastward

Then at the end of 1894 the pressure shifted to a thriving Seventh-day Adventist community in East Tennessee with a new school called Graysville Academy. In March, 1895 the Grand Jury handed down 77 indictments, 31 of which charged Graysville Adventists with breaking the Sunday laws.

Entitling the story "Adventist in prison," the March 26, 1895 *Review* ran an account of their situation as published in the Chicago *Inter Ocean* and written by the editor of the Dayton *Republican*.

"Graysville, Tenn. is a rural community of five or six hundred people five miles from Dayton, the county seat, in Rhea County. What distinguishes Graysville above any other town in East Tennessee, and will make it noted throughout the country, is that at least one fifth of the town is composed of Seventh-day Adventists, who just now are undergoing a legal persecution because of their peculiar faith.

"Some twenty of these Adventists have been tried in the Rhea County Circuit Court the past week on the charge of violating the Sunday law of the State by working on this day. . . The Adventists . . . are enthusiasts in their belief, and are willing to suffer persecution for the truth's sake, as they view it. Nearly all of the week has been consumed in these trials, and the court-room has been crowded by interested spectators, some of them coming from as far as New York. For once the lawyers took a back seat, as the Adventists conducted their own cases. They made no legal defense, indulged in no quibbles, and did not attempt to shield themselves behind any technicalities. Each of the accused parties was armed with a Bible, however, and with this religious weapon they attempted to combat the carnal operations of the law. Vain effort. The law has no spiritual sense, and the unsophisticated children of God were routed and their banner of faith torn down.

"The Adventists are not dismayed, however, and will meekly submit to their punishment, which is imprisonment in the county workhouse until their fines are worked out; for one of the peculiarities of these people is that they will not pay a fine, as they thereby concede the rights of the civil law to interfere with their religion. Judge Parks, in reviewing the case, said that he was sorry that it was his painful duty to find the defendants guilty, but that as the law on the question of Sunday observance was unequivocal, and that, as his was a temporal and not a spiritual court, it could not do otherwise. He fined each of the convicted parties $2.50 and costs, and immediately remitted the fine, but said that it was not in his power to remit the costs.

"The scenes in court during the progress of the trial were characteristic. Elder Colcord, the leader of the devoted band, made an earnest and fervid plea, based upon the Bible largely. At the same time he claimed that the Sunday law of Tennessee was unconstitutional, and made some very good arguments from this standpoint. The elder is a spare-built, stoop-shouldered man of about 60 years, with a patriarchal beard and an ascetic countenance. His appearance in the midst of his persecutors put one forcibly in mind of Paul before Agrippa, or to make a stronger metaphor, of Daniel in the lions' den.

"The conviction and the punishment of these people will seriously affect the prosperity of their community at Graysville. One of the convicted parties, Professor Colcord, a brother of the elder, has been conducting a very successful school, which is now broken up. The informant in these cases is one Wright Raines, a dissolute coal miner."

This editor went on to note that "There are about forty thousand Adventists in the United States. They have a number of publishing houses, do an extensive foreign work and are pushing the work of proselytizing at home. They are earnest and zealous and are with us to stay. What are we going to do with them? Are we going to persecute them as were the Christian martyrs during the Middle Ages? To be sure the fire and the faggot have gone out of fashion, but we still have the rock pile and ball and chain. The question is one of national interest. As yet the Supreme Court of the United States has not passed upon the constitutionality of Sunday laws. The Adventists had one case pending before that tribunal, but the man died before the august judges reached it.

"I am not an Adventist, but I believe in the fullest exercise of the individual conscience on matters of religion, and the entire separation of Church and State. The State has no right to dictate to a man his mode or manner of worship, so long as he does not transgress the spiritual rights or moral laws of man or God.

"In the meantime, while these questions are being debated, good Elder Colcord will lie in Rhea County jail 200 days, as much a martyr to the fanaticism of this 19th century as were Bruno and Galileo during what we are pleased to term the Dark Ages."

After profiling the larger work of Adventists, the editor noted that "The school at Graysville was established by Elder Colcord in 1892. It has grown and prospered until closed by these Sunday persecutions. It has an enrollment of over one hundred. A comfortable school building has been erected, as has also been a boarding house and dormitory.

"The Adventists do not, as some have supposed, court persecution. They have exhausted every legal remedy in this State, except it might be as an appeal to the Supreme Court of the United States. They refuse to pay fines, because to do so would be to acknowledge the justice of their conviction. They do not take a very cheerful view of the future from a human standpoint, believing that Sunday laws, instead of being modified, will be made more rigorous, and that persecution, instead of being confined to a few states as at present, will become world-wide, and will be terminated only by the end of the world, which they believe is not far distant, though they are not of the number who set a time for that event.

"Altogether they are an interesting people, and the majority of the citizens of Rhea County greatly regret that they cannot be permitted to pursue their work at Graysville uninterruptedly. The school has certainly been a benefit to this community, and aside from their Sunday work they are law-abiding people and excellent citizens."

Judge Parker himself admitted that he disagreed with the law and disliked having to fine these Adventists. "If I were to express my private feelings, however, I might say that there is nothing I regard with more concern or solicitude than an encroachment of legislative enactment upon the personal rights of the individual in matters of conscience," he remarked in court. "That there is a limit in these matters beyond which legislation cannot rightfully go will be conceded by every man. Where is that limit?"

The March 26, 1895 *Review* announced that the indictment, arrests, and jailing of Elder G.W. Colcord, principal; Professor I.C. Colcord, one of the teachers; and M.C. Sturdevant, boys' dean had forced a closing of Graysville Academy. Other people jailed with them were William and Henry Burchard, Dwight Plumb, W.J. Kerr, E.S. Abbott, William Wolf, N.B. England, E.M. Plumb, A.F. Harrison, and B.L. Dieffenbacher.

All, with the exception of William Wolf, whose father secured his costs, refused to pay their fine and were therefore sentenced from 20 to 80 days in prison including Wolf. Their defense was the God-given right to work six days of the week.

Judge James G. Parks charged the jury to uphold the law of the State of Tennessee.

"Peculiar interest attaches to the cases of the Seventh-day Adventists, because this persecution directly affects Graysville Academy, which is closed indefinitely because of the imprisonment of the principal and the teacher second in charge," commented the *Review*. "It works a special hardship upon some of the students who were almost ready to graduate, and who are now compelled to return to their homes at considerable expense, without finishing their course at school. Most of the students are scattered to various States, and others are awaiting the receipt of money from home, to enable them to leave." The article also pointed out that all but one of the imprisoned men had families back home depending upon them for their security.

W.W. Prescott, president of Battle Creek College, visited Graysville and reported a "peculiar" situation in the *Review*. A local ne'er-do-well had apparently brought the charges against these Adventists, reminding Prescott of a Thomas Jefferson quote. "The spirit of the times may alter, will alter . . . A single zealot may commence persecution, and better men be his victims."

Prescott reported talking with the judge and attorneys involved, saying they all disagreed with what had happened, but the men were still in jail. He and Brother A.R. Henry, a top administrator at the Review and Herald Publishing House, met with the prisoners and reported a good spirit among them. But he saw no end in sight for their release or for the reopening of Graysville Academy.

Prescott called a public meeting, and a large crowd came out to a public hall in Dayton, Tennessee. He explained why Seventh-day

Adventists refused to obey Sunday laws and would rather suffer imprisonment rather than pay a nominal fine. He reported an excellent attendance, with some professional people from the community composing part of the audience.

"I spent the Sabbath with the church at Graysville," Prescott wrote. "The pastor, one of the elders, a deacon, the superintendent of the Sabbath School, and the chorister are in jail (a bad record on the face of it, but an honor to the church when the circumstances are all known), but the brethren and sisters are of good courage and do not show any inclination to compromise the truth but rather to do as 'aforetime.' It was touching and encouraging to hear wives whose husbands were in jail, speak of their hope and courage in the Lord.

"The imprisoned brethren continue in good health and are of excellent courage. At our farewell service with them last Sunday afternoon, we sang 'God Be with you till we meet again,' while tears of sympathy freely flowed. The Lord is fulfilling to them his promise that 'as thy days, so shall thy strength be,' and they are content 'in behalf of Christ, not only to believe on him but also to suffer for his sake.'"

The church petitioned the Rhea County Court regarding the Sunday laws, but 15 out of 29 justices of the peace turned it down.

Then someone introduced a bill into the Tennessee State Legislature making all property subject to execution in case of conviction for a misdemeanor. Apparently the expense of incarcerating all these people for violating Sunday laws in these counties had become an issue, and the state thought to cover the imprisonment expenses by confiscating wearing apparel, household goods, etc.

This bill failed to pass.

The next arrest occurred in the Roane County town of Harriman, Tennessee. A policeman spotted J.B. Thayer planting potatoes on his land and summoned him to court the next day.

Harassment Backfires

These arrests and imprisonments were beginning to hurt the image of Tennessee. A letter to the editor of the Dayton (Tenn.) *Republican* summed up the situation.

"Has it ever occurred to you what the effect of this religious persecution in Tennessee will have on immigration?" wrote a John Hamilton Davis. "If not, I can tell you.

"I have just returned from a nine months' visit to Ohio, where I found, scattered everywhere among the farmers, copies of the *American Sentinel* and other papers, giving full account of the imprisonment of the Adventists in Rhea County, Tennessee. In one settlement a number of farmers had made up their minds to move to Tennessee, and had formed a club for that purpose.

"But this religious persecution knocked the whole thing in the head. The majority of these intending immigrants were Republicans, and they feared to move South. Said one of them to me:

"'The old rebel spirit is just as rampant in the South as ever, and I am not going where there is no religious or political freedom. If the Tennessee authorities persecute and imprison men and women for their religious belief, they would find some pretext to harass and persecute me, because I am a Republican, and the rest who would go there. No, sir, I am not going to such a State. I tell you we are not going to such a place. I see that they also imprison Adventists in Georgia, and I guess it is the same way all over the South.'

"Thousands of people at the North want to come South, but they are afraid of religious or political persecution. Many of the old prejudices against the South had worn away, and there was a feeling of confidence in East Tennessee, with its big Republican majority, but the recent persecution of Christians in Rhea County and the counting out of G.H. Clay Evans, have retarded immigration—set it back for years,--and unless the intolerant laws there are repealed, and a free and honest ballot maintained, the State will lose millions in immigration.

"As a Southerner who loves the South, and wants to see it grow in population and in wealth, I am sorry to see such a state of things. There are thousands of Adventists and Seventh-day Baptists in the Northern and Western States, who observe the Seventh day, but not the first day of the week; but not one of these people has ever been arrested or in any way molested because of his religious belief. To do such a thing is a crime against freedom, a violation of the Constitution, of man. It is a monstrous act of injustice, for which Tennessee must surely suffer in loss of immigration, as I have already pointed out.

"I am not an Adventist. I have nothing in common with these people except a desire for liberty of thought. But I have lived among these people, mingled with them, and know that if there are any conscientious, honest, truly religious and really worthy people and patriotic citizens, they will be found among the Adventists.

"And to see other so-called Christians persecuting them, and informing on them, and backing up the authorities who send the Adventists to jail simply because they do not believe as the other Christians believe, is simply a horrible and contemptible mockery on religion. The Christian who would imprison another Christian because of a difference in belief, is not a Christian, but a devil incarnate. Why, if this thing keeps up, we may look for a re-establishment of the Inquisition with all its bloody horrors!

"All laws conflicting with perfect religious freedom, not only in Tennessee, but in all the Southern States, should be repealed, and laws enacted granting persons the right to worship and work as their consciences dictate. We want perfect mental, religious, and political liberty. Our forefathers fought for these things. But if good people are to be imprisoned because of their religious belief, then our forefathers fought in vain, and liberty is a mockery and a lie."

The June 11, 1895 *Review* reported that Gov. Peter Turney had pardoned the imprisoned Graysville Adventists. He had regarded it as his duty to uphold the Sunday laws as Chief Justice of the Supreme Court, having heard the Parker and King cases. But now, as governor, he exercised his prerogative to void penalties he himself regarded as unjust. The article added that this act of the governor, however, did not end the prosecution of Adventists in the court system. "Quite a number more, however, were indicted and will be tried at the next term of court," wrote A.O. Tait.

"A petition is being circulated among the citizens in the vicinity of Graysville, asking that the Sunday law be still more rigidly enforced," he continued. "Our correspondent informs us that our people there are surprised to see the names of some citizens affixed to it that they had considered quite favorable toward us. Notwithstanding this, others are being made acquainted with the prophecies for these times, and are seeing how rapidly things are developing."

This next court found nine Rhea County Adventists guilty and fined them from $5 to $15 plus court costs. For technical reasons, two of the cases were postponed, two defendants found not guilty, and one case involving a small boy was thrown out of court.

"The judge in his sentence stated very clearly that he was sorry that it was necessary for him to prosecute the brethren," wrote A.O. Tait. "He believed they were good, law-abiding citizens, and that it was too bad that they had to be treated in this way.

But he said that as long as the law stood the way it does, his oath of office placed him under obligation to enforce the law."

The good news, according to Tait, was that "the arrests of these brethren are being reported through the papers, and a good deal of discussion is being had because of it.

Our literature has been placed in a large number of homes in Tennessee during the last few weeks. These reports are creating a healthy interest in the study of the truth, and some are being led to take their stand in favor of it."

Indeed, J.M. Hall telegraphed to the *Review* on July 22, 1895, that 50 people had called on him and his fellow prisoners the day before and the Lord had helped his brethren to talk His truth. "You say, 'Courage in the Lord'; we say, 'Praise the Lord.'"

Their punishment was hard. D.W. Reavis wrote in the July 30, 1895, *Review* that the Adventists on the chain gang in Spring City, Tennessee, refused to work on Sabbath with the other local criminals and paid for it by not allowing the Sabbath day count towards their time in jail.

"They must have that day counted out of their time, and if reports are true, they must also pay for their board on that day," Reavis wrote. "This is the first step toward compelling our people to work on the Sabbath. Public sentiment will allow this step, and through it will become hardened for a more severe punishment next time, and erelong the people of America will look upon the punishment of Adventists as calmly as they behold the punishment of a thief."

Reavis added that the local authorities had placed a young man refusing to work with the chain gang on Sabbath in an upper room and allowed him only bread and water during the day.

"In these cases the real issue is clearly seen," Reavis continued. "It is not Sunday-breaking but Sabbath-keeping for which our people suffer. All the other prisoners in the gang, except our people, have not only violated the Sunday laws, but are criminals in strictly civil things, and yet they are held in favor above our people. In Dayton, where our people were imprisoned, 500 people do unnecessary work every Sunday, and no one is molested for it, because they keep no other day. But because our people keep the Sabbath, they are very offensive in the sight of the people when they work on Sunday, and this hatred is not even satisfied when they get them in the chain gang. The most vile wretch upon the face of the earth is preferred and favored rather than a moral man whose sole offense in the sight of men is his refusing to sacrifice his conscience."

The next month, the *Review* ran a picture of the "The Chain Gang at work," three criminals and seven Adventists: H.C. Leach, W.J. Kerr, Monroe Morgan, J.M. Hall, W.S. Burchard, Dwight Plumb and Byrd Terry.

The fellow soldiers of chain gang member E.R. Gillett, who had served with him during the Civil War, regarded his sentence as being an "undeserved indignity."

"We, survivors of the Ninety-ninth and other regiments of Illinois troops, at or near Nebo, Pike County, Illinois, assembled in reunion on this 23rd day of August, 1895, do most emphatically object to such treatment of our comrade, and earnestly request that justice be done to one who has so dearly earned his liberty by exposing his life 'neath the stars and stripes in the hours of his country's peril."

"Though there is not a general uprising among the people in Tennessee against working men in the chain-gang for conscience' sake, there is a deep consideration of the principles involved among the best element of society throughout the South," wrote D.W. Reavis in the *Review*. "While it is evident that the people will soon become accustomed to the severe punishment of Adventists for their faith, it is also demonstrated that those who are susceptible to the truth are accepting it as such,--though many, at present, by mere assent of the mind,--yet some are adopting it as their faith. The Sabbath, its observance, and its relation to the civil government, is fast becoming a very popular topic for discussion by individuals, the pulpit, and the press; and every attempt to justify the observance of Sunday, either by the Scriptures or the civil law, results in a signal defeat, and a triumph for the true Sabbath."

Reavis also pointed out that Seventh-day believers in Georgia and Mississippi faced the same legal challenges as those in Rhea County.

Positive Results

But draconian punishment failed to suppress Adventism. R.M. Kilgore reported erecting a tent and starting evangelistic meetings in Spring City, a town of 700 people and home to the chain gang organizer and site where the chain gang was assigned to work. "They (chain gang members) are allowed the privilege of attending the night meetings, but last Sabbath they were prohibited from leaving their quarters.

"We find sympathizing friends here who are ashamed of this treatment of our brethren," Kilgore continued. "Friday night our congregation numbered about 60, and on Sunday night it was over 200. Some of the ministers are doing all they can to keep their people away from the tent. The Lord gives freedom to his servants." A few months later, Elder Smith Sharp reported that six or eight had embraced Adventism.

The chain gang episode became part of a special issue of the General Conference-produced *American Sentinel*, also featuring past persecutions in Spain, France, and the Netherlands.

An Era Starts to Close

Then the chain gang sentence ended. "The authorities turned brethren Leach, Terry, and me loose yesterday," wrote W.S. Burchard to D.W. Reavis. "The time of all the others is out today, except brother Plumb's. All will help him put some time in, and he will be out in a day or two.

"We all come out sound and well. The Lord has been with us, and given us strength to go through. We have been able to work all the time, except Brother Terry; he had the toothache about half a day. All the other prisoners I think have been sick more or less.

"So this ends this term of chain-gang life, and we can all praise God for his goodness and blessings through it. I hope it will cause some honest souls to see and accept the truth.

"We are fully able to go up and possess the goodly land. I do not think that one of us is sorry that we have been permitted to have this experience."

"There is something pathetic in the fact that one of their number was required to remain in the chain gang for a longer time than the rest, and so upon their release they voluntarily remained in the chain gang to assist him in working out his time so that they could all go home together," wrote A.O. Tait in the September 10, 1895 *Review*. "Any State, if it was not blinded by religious prejudice or bigotry, could see the farce of calling such men criminals."

Tait also called attention to Adventist believers facing similar punishments in Ontario and Georgia. "Brethren and sisters, these times in which we are living are filled with interest," Tait concluded. "Do we sense how rapidly the signs of the times are fulfilling? And are we so devoting ourselves to the work that when the Master comes, and his coming can be but a little ways off, he will say to us the welcome words, 'Well done'?"

But though the chain gang members were out of jail, they were not yet out of trouble. D.W. Reavis reported that the local authorities told some of them they would have to make up the days they had lost while on Sabbath furlough or down sick, a sentence not imposed on the everyday offenders in jail. "The reason for this is, evidently, to force our people into the observance of Sunday; for they are repeatedly threatened with the full penalty of the law if they come to the chain gang again," Reavis concluded.

But then the political climate seemed to change.

An article from the November 6, 1895, Chattanooga *Times* indicated that these Rhea County persecutions were over for the time being. "Today the last of the Adventist cases was swept from the docket, and appearances indicate that the wave of fanaticism and prejudice which has been sweeping over Rhea County has subsided," the paper reported.

The article went on to say that the cases of Wallace Ridgeway, N.B. England, and Civil War veteran E.R. Gillett were dismissed from court, thanks to an effective defense by ex-Congressman H.C. Snodgrass of Sparta and Judge Lewis Shepherd of Chattanooga.

"Many things have occurred recently to bring the question of what are called the Sunday laws prominently before the people," the *Times* concluded editorially. "In New York the question is one of the indirect issues in the election occurring yesterday, and in various of the larger cities it is being mooted with the more or less vigor. To come nearer home, in Dayton, Tenn., a number of the class known as Seventh-day Adventists are being made the victims of a conflict between conscience and the State law on the subject of Sunday observance, and in such a manner, too, and on such provocation as to appear very much like persecution. These people are known and acknowledged to be good citizens, God-fearing, industrious, and law-abiding, save where their consciences and their religious beliefs conflict with what they conceive to be unjust legislation. While no one can or will censure the court for enforcing the law against these people, when an infraction is brought to its notice, there is much to say why such infractions should not be dealt with as in the case of malicious and willful violations by men who not only have no conscientious scruples against the observance of the day, but who have no consciences at all."

"Every friend of civil and religious liberty will rejoice in the finding of the Tennessee jury in favor of the Adventists who were arrested on a charge of Sabbath-breaking," wrote the Chicago *Inter Ocean*. "It is part of the creed of the Adventists, as of the Drunkards, the Quakers, the Mennonites and some other singularly pure-lived sects, 'not to resist evil by evil.' Some of them carry this maxim so far as to endure arrest and confiscation of goods rather than to employ lawyers to defend them. However, in this Tennessee case, a Congressman and a former judge volunteered appearance as *amioi curie* and, in telling speeches, argued for dismissal of the cases. The trial judge instructed the jury to acquit, and an acquittal followed."

And that seemed to end the trials, but the last reference to them in the *Review* showed that the King case in Obion County had left its mark. The

April 26, 1898 edition published a letter from a Thomas W. Winn, writing from Covington, Tennessee, telling how he became an Adventist through the legal ordeals of Brother King at the beginning of the decade.

"It was my good fortune to serve on the grand jury of the United States Circuit Court when this case came up for investigation," he wrote. "The case was argued at considerable length by different jurors, some holding that Sunday was the Lord's day, and should be observed because God had so commanded, and a few claiming that Saturday was the seventh day, and, consequently, ought to be observed as the Sabbath. Not being well informed in the law of God on the subject, but having read the constitution of Tennessee, I argued from a constitutional standpoint that the fundamental law of the State guaranteed to every citizen the right to serve God according to the dictates of his own conscience, and that the constitutional law of a State was paramount to any statutory law that might or could be enacted by the legislature of the State.

"This noted trial was the beginning of my investigation of the Scriptures, in order to ascertain if the keeping of Sunday was in accordance with the law of God. From time to time I would study the subject a while, and then think, Can it be that my ancestors for generations back have committed so grave an error as to overlook this express command of the great Jehovah? Certainly they could not. Then I would drop the subject for a time, and go about my secular affairs. But Brother King's case kept coming up in my mind, and after a while (by accident, I came near saying, but I do not think it was an accident), a friend handed to me *The Marvel of Nations*, by Uriah Smith, which I read and reread with the most intense interest. Then I began to see what God had commanded in regard to this matter, and was "almost persuaded" to keep the Sabbath, when Brother J.D. Pegg came here to hold a series of meetings. By his presentation of logical arguments and deductions, I, with a number of others, became fully convinced that the seventh day is the day that God requires shall be kept as his holy Sabbath. Last Sabbath, in accordance with our convictions, we organized a Sabbath School, which I feel satisfied will be well attended."

So the fiery trials of the 1890s brought the church and its message to the attention of a general public that would otherwise have learned little or nothing about Adventism. Missionary work among friends and neighbors continued, but that never attracted national attention. These struggling new Adventist converts made more impact than the more established and respectable Christians.

Later Important Workers

E.E. Marvin

E.E. Marvin was ordained to the Adventist ministry in Logansport, Indiana, in 1885 at the age of 31. Health problems threatened to shorten his life, and a serious crisis inspired him to enter the gospel ministry. Hard work in the Indiana climate adversely affected him, so he transferred to warmer Tennessee.

His first dispatch to the Review came out in 1887, describing a small group in Corinth, just outside of Portland, Tennessee, as being "in a discouraged condition, not having had any meetings for several months." The people there had faced bitter opposition, with some of their neighbors trying unsuccessfully to persuade the local Grand Jury to indict them. Though their enemies had laid them low, Marvin felt his visit inspired them to begin anew.

He then went over to Springfield, "one of the greatest whisky and tobacco centers in the State," and attracted "the best class of citizens," to his meetings, according to an article in the same Review.

"Theater and prohibition meetings almost broke up our interest several times, yet a few came out almost every night," he wrote. "With but very few exceptions, all agree that we have the truth; but the cross seems too heavy for many of them to lift."

He next went to Gleason in Weakly County. "We tried the plan of presenting the Sabbath question as soon as we had introduced the papacy, and by so doing we were enabled to get the Sabbath before large crowds," he reported. "We are now explaining the prophecies, and still the attendance is good. We like the plan."

Fellow minister J.M. Rees reported Marvin to be in failing health there, yet Marvin stayed with his work and got results. "The mass of the people are convinced that the seventh-day is the Sabbath of the Lord," he wrote. "The ministers of the place are uneasy because of the interest taken in our meetings." He closed at Gleason with a dozen or so people keeping the Sabbath.

The Leach church in the fall of 1887 reported some apostasies among the new converts. Several resolved to resume paying tithe.

In 1888, he assumed greater leadership as J.M. Rees departed to help develop the infant cause in North Carolina. Marvin started the year by holding meetings in McKenzie. From there he went to Lane. "I found them all firm in the truth and exhibiting commendable missionary zeal," he wrote. He went on to the Center church, Cross Plains and the Ridge, and then found about a dozen Sabbath keepers in Columbia. Thanks to an influential man named Dr. W.C. Sheppard, he had the use of a centralized lot in town rent free. Adventism still struggled in Franklin and Corinth, but a large audience turned out to listen to him at Ridge.

Marvin felt that the violence and persecution breaking out in Lane had a lot to do with two prominent citizens accepting Adventism there, and he reported that small group working hard on a new church building.

Springfield, Corinth and Ridge all demanded his time. Then in 1889 he went to Graysville and found a live group of believers, many of whom had moved there from the north. Jackson, Tennessee, had a population of about 12,000 people and two or three families accepting Adventism.

The December 17, 1889, Review listed him as president of the Tennessee River Conference, and he announced two general meetings, one in Springville and the other in Central Kentucky.

Meetings at Leach, Carter's School House and Springville followed, and then it was back to Cross Plains. "Some unpleasantness has existed for about two years, among some of the members of this church," he wrote. "This we have tried to remove, and have reason to hope that if all promises are faithfully kept, in the future this evil will not be found in this church."

He found good interest in Center, 11 miles from Springfield, Keysburgh, Leitchfield, Kentucky, and Hamilton, Kentucky, virgin territory with no prior Adventist influence.

He called for a general meeting in Bowling, Green, Kentucky.

Then he worked the Tennessee circuit of Nashville, Columbia, Edgefield Junction and Daysville as well as Leach and Springville.

In summing up all the court cases going on at this time, he wrote in the July 29, 1890, Review that "the recent demonstrations of hatred against us and our work have by no means discouraged our people. The inquisitors seem to be waiting for something. They are doubtless beginning to learn that they have a larger job on their hands than they at first imagined."

He reported the Henry County Grand Jury awaiting the Supreme Court decision on the King appeal, assuming they would want to put others through the same ordeal. He also thanked believers in other states for their support of the Tennessee brethren under duress.

He wrote that he had organized the Lane Church three years before (1887) with four members, with R.M. King as elder since he was the only male member. Threats of violence had scared many people away, "but those who love the truth were by no means frightened away," he wrote. "Two took a stand for the truth at this meeting, one was baptized, and three were received into the church."

Lane now had 13 members, and he reported three families of Sabbath-keepers in Mt. Pelia.

Delegates from Cross Plains, Springville and Trezevant came to the tenth annual session of the Tennessee River Conference in 1890. Leach, Ridge, Center, Lane and Edgefield Junction, Tennessee, church representatives did not show up. The Bowling Green, Rio, Leitchfield and Russellville, Kentucky, church delegates also missed the meeting, with the session voting to disband the Russellville Church.

Soon after, following a Southern Council in Atlanta, Elder Marvin caught "quick consumption" and died in December, 1890, at his home in Trezevant, Tennessee, at the age of 36 years, 2 months and 24 days old according to his *Review* obituary.

H.W. Reed

In the June 16, 1891, edition of the *Review*, H.W. Reed described Bowling Green, Kentucky, as a progressive county seat with "several commodious churches of various denominations, but no public worship place for the few Seventh-day Adventist believers there. They are forced to meet in a crowded private house," he wrote. "What an opening is this for some of our brethren of Battle Creek, and other large churches, to move in here, and set on foot the erection of a church, and thus give some stability and permanence to the work."

Rees added that the conference did not own a church building in all of Western Kentucky, "and I have been informed that in the same district there are only about four organized churches, of a dozen members or less. How destitute is this field, of God's remnant people. May God move upon some who are dying spiritually for lack of an opportunity to do missionary work, to move into Bowling Green, and other cities and towns of this field nearly destitute of believers in the third angel's message!"

Rees added in his first account of labor in this new field that the Bowling Green members had supported the general meeting held there but only three showed up from the distant churches, one of whom joined through baptism.

"I understand that there are less than 50 Sabbath keepers in all of Western Kentucky," he concluded. "We pray that God will help us to so labor that we may gather sheaves for the garner of heaven."

The annual Tennessee River Conference session the following October elected Reed Secretary pro tem in the absence of the regular conference secretary. The churches in Springville, Leach, Rio, Edgefield Junction, Cross Plains, Lane, Bowling Green, Trazevant and Nashville sent delegates.

Elder C.M. Kinney reported organizing a black church in Bowling Green with eight members. Brother J.H. Dortch moved that the conference accept it.

In his next dispatch to the Review on February 14, 1893, Reed reported good meetings in Springville, Gardner, Martin, McKenzie, Trezevant, Leach and Lane, Tennessee.

From Hazel, Kentucky, he gladly reported that a Dr. Mason and his family had remained faithful after accepting Adventism the year before. Their sons had since accepted Adventism and Dr. Mason's son-in-law had made a big impact on the community by taking his stand and closing his two stores on the Sabbath.

"In conclusion, I can say that I have enjoyed much of God's power in presenting the truth for this time," he summed up. "And as I have received new light and life and power from above, how my own heart has longed that others should feel this heavenly power. If no other work was assigned me, I should like to travel from church to church, following much the same course as is seen by this report."

He experienced persecution firsthand while preaching 22 sermons during 18 days in Plano, Ky. "The prejudice became quite strong, so much so that I was locked out of the school-house," he said. "After this someone one wrote an anonymous letter to a prominent business man of the place, bemeaning the people of Plano. This was laid to me. Threats were made that 'if I came back there again, they would treat me worse than they had already done.' How plainly the spirit of the dragon is manifested nowadays."

Reed kept up his pace, visiting the Rio church in Kentucky, then Bowling Green, still having a church organization but no building. He later preached six sermons in a large church in Dickson, Tennessee, at the request of the pastor and trustees until the church members requested that he leave.

Reed spent 29 days in Girkin, Kentucky, with five people taking their stand.

In an article datelined Knoxville, Tennessee, Reed wrote that "We were greatly surprised and gratified to find as much ability and culture among the colored population as we did. They are higher than we had been led to think. The masses seem wholly given up to pleasure-seeking, but here and there among them are those who sigh and cry on account of the abominations done in their midst."

He told two inspiring conversion stories of black converts and the serious attempts made to undermine their faith, and reported a company of eight Sabbath keepers and a Sabbath School with a membership of 15.

He ended 1893 by preaching 26 times in the great spiritual battlefield of Lane, paying tribute to the now deceased R.M. King.

"Only one mile from the church is the spot where our much esteemed brother slumbers, awaiting the voice of the Life giver to awaken him out of sleep," he wrote. "Brother King was a man of great moral courage. Shortly before he died, he said: 'I would rather die than break God's Sabbath,' and his subsequent life and death proved that he meant what he said."

"A few rods away from bother King's resting place stands the school house that was fired into by a mob while Elder William Covert was preaching some years ago. This mob fired fifteen or twenty shots with the intention to kill. Some of the most active leaders in this religious Kuklux mob, organized to exterminate the work there, have passed from life's scenes, and are sleeping in the same cemetery with brother King. While I was there, one was interred in this cemetery, whom our brethren have reasons to believe was conspicuous in that mob. Thus do they die without making confession of their murderous intent."

The Lane church had some strong believers, with one of their members, L.A. Callicott, a member of the Conference Committee.

His June 26, 1894, report showed him hoping to organize a church in Oliver Springs, Tennessee, going nearby to conduct meetings in Webster, Indian Creek, and then Middle Creek.

Basing himself in Nashville, Reed made another excursion to the churches in Trezevant and Leach, preaching 17 times and baptizing nine people.

He wrote that Marion, Kentucky, had had just one Adventist for the past nine years, but 10 had started keeping the Sabbath after some meetings he conducted there. Memphis, Tennessee, was starting to open up for Adventism as the result of much book distribution.

He began meetings in historic Murfreesboro, Tennessee, on May 5, 1896, in a 50-foot tent only one block from the square, preaching 71 sermons.

"During our stay in Murfreesboro, we have had several pleasant calls from ex-Senator W.OP. Tolley, who is a staunch friend of Seventh-day Adventists because of their correct views of religious liberty, with which he is in harmony," Reed wrote. "He gave us a hearty invitation to visit him at his home, which we did. Our prayer is that the day will come when he will not only be a *friend* of the persecuted, but be *one* of them."

According to his obituary, malaria caused H.W. Reed to leave Tennessee for Wisconsin in 1897. He later worked in California, dying at Healdsburg in 1924.

Charles L. Boyd

During his stay in Tennessee, Reed worked under a conference president named Charles L. Boyd.

In his first report in the Review, on June 30, 1891, Boyd wrote that the Cross Plains people worshiped in the "union church" and that Springville was the largest church in the Tennessee River Conference.

"The state agent and several of the canvassers reside here," he wrote. "The parents and family of Brother Bollman, associate editor of the Sentinel, have recently moved to this neighborhood."

"Among other places, I expect to visit Dyer County, where our people have suffered so much persecution for the truth's sake," he continued. "But public sentiment is changing. Northern people are coming South, where they can enjoy a milder climate, and a mutual benefit is the result of the association of the different classes."

He visited the Lane Church, "the house where a volley of bullets was fired at Brother Covert and the congregation who were listening to his preaching," and found them now worshiping in "a neat chapel of their own."

The court decision regarding the Sunday law violation of R.M. King was still pending, and the church members attended his meetings "without fear."

He described Columbia, Tennessee, as "one of the most beautiful and healthy towns that I have ever seen in the south. May the time soon come when a goodly number will be found here keeping all of the commandments of God and the faith of Jesus."

The September annual session of the Tennessee River Conference, held in connection with the camp meeting in McKenzie, Tennessee, appointed Elder Boyd as president pro tem due to the death of E.E. Marvin. Nine registered delegates represented the Springville, Cross Plains and Rio churches.

He then conducted meetings in Nashville and Dickson County in response to a man there who had started keeping the seventh-day Sabbath completely on his own.

Springville seemed to be his center of activity, with the persecution dying down. Prominent Adventist minister A.T. Jones joined him in Nashville to protest the "Sunday exemption bill" to the state legislature.

"A favorable opportunity was thus afforded to present the principles of religious liberty before the representative men of the State," he wrote. "A radical change has taken place in the minds of many leading men here, for which we thank God and take courage. I have since met the governor of the State, and consider him favorable to religious liberty, and familiar with our literature whose principles are so ably advocated."

He made repeated pleas to Battle Creek believers to come south and use their influence in places with no Adventist presence at all.

In the February 20, 1894, Review, Elder Boyd described the Graysville school as prospering under the care of Professor W.C. Colcord and his faithful fellow-teachers."

He went on to Lexington, Kentucky, to "a small company of refined and intelligent colored people who have taken their stand for the truths of the gospel; others are seriously considering such a stand under the labors of brother and sister A. Barry."

He organized a Sabbath School with 15 members there and appointed a treasurer to collect the tithes.

He described Lexington as "a thriving city of 35,000 inhabitants. It has a pleasant and healthful situation. We would invite some good families who desire to engage in self-supporting home missionary work in a fruitful field and congenial climate to come this way."

He regretted that Guthrie, Kentucky, had no members despite the conference having conducted two camp meetings there.

The West Tennessee believers still faced serious opposition. He reported W.B. Capps, a member of the Trezevant church, "now under bonds to appear at the supreme court of the State. One year ago he was found guilty by the circuit court of violating the sanctity of the Roman Sabbath."

Then something he regarded as providential happened. The lower court clerk lost the papers to the Capps case, delaying the Supreme Court hearing.

"Now is an unfavorable time to bring this testing question before this honorable body, as they are absorbed in matters of election," he concluded.

He went on to Obion County and still felt the influence of the failed attempt to stamp out Adventism.

"Here is the home of our late beloved brother R.M. King," he wrote. "Here stands the schoolhouse into which some 20 shots were fired while Elder Covert was teaching that men ought rather to keep the "commandments of God" than the commandments of men. Since coming here I have been treated with courtesy by the people; the meetings have been quite well attended, and it has been my privilege to baptize four willing souls. Three of these are adults who have but recently commenced to observe the Sabbath. Several others are keeping the Sabbath who we hope will soon be prepared to be identified with those whom the Lord is clothing with the righteousness of God."

Boyd reported conducting a successful series of meetings at Bowling Green with H.W. Reed resulting in 18 people joining the church. He also praised the work of literature evangelists, saying hard economic times favoring the Adventists because all but the dedicated workers had given up.

In the January 1, 1895, *Review*, Elder Boyd sensed possibilities in Hazel, Kentucky, a town that would become an important center for the Tennessee River Conference in the years to come. He reported conducting services in the Baptist church there and celebrating the Lord's Supper with a group of believers in the home of Dr. W.M. Mason. "May the time soon come when a church can be organized at Hazel," he wrote. "This is a new town, and the company here are very anxious to have one or more families of good Seventh-day Adventists move in and unite with them in their work and service."

Then it was on to Columbia, Tennessee, then Bowling Green and Linwood, Kentucky. By mid-1895, he reported a small company of Sabbath keepers in Marion, Kentucky, things looking up with a new brick building under construction in Bowling Green and a new 20-member Sabbath School in nearby Sand Hill, Kentucky. People moving away had depleted the Cross Plains, Tennessee, church, but Edgefield Junction was building. The Nashville Church was struggling and recently joined two congregations of different races into one. He was just starting work in McEwen, Tennessee, with a Nashville Adventist family having just moved there.

Elder Boyd really liked Watertown, Tennessee, "a pleasant village in a fine farming country, between 40 and 50 miles east of Nashville. The country for many miles around is awakened by this gospel truth. I have never before seen such an interest in Tennessee. Last night the seats in our 50-foot tent were full, and many people stood." He had an equally good experience in nearby Alexandria, but noted while the people were under conviction, it was still too soon to see if they would actually live their newly-found faith long-term.

He ended 1895 in Memphis, reporting a newly-organized church with 10 members. "At this writing I am on my way to Lake County, where Brother Lewis is under bonds for refusing to 'receive the mark of the beast.' I had the privilege of baptizing this brother one year ago this month. . . . I am now in Obion County, near the house where Elder Covert and his congregation were fired upon by a mob of some 20 Christians(?)."

In a later article he reported five church members, two of them elders, under arrest and facing a court trial in Lake County. Cross Plains seemed fine, and something was starting in Murfreesboro and Ashland City. The Corinth Church merged with Cross Plains.

Elder Boyd relinquished his work as president at the 1896 Tennessee River Conference constituency meeting but

Dr. W.M. Mason of Hazel, Kentucky, accepted Adventism in 1893 and operated a sanitarium. An Adventist academy then developed here, and Hazel became the scene of important conference meetings early in the 20th century. Two generations of Masons served as physicians there and later in the county seat of Murray, Kentucky.

still stayed on and started a series of meetings in Clarksville, Tennessee, and later at Paducah, Kentucky.

"To the friends who are inquiring the reason of my silence through the *Review*, I would say that during the past few months my health has not been good, and consequently my time has not been fully spent in the harvest field," he wrote in the August 3, 1897, *Review*. "Nevertheless, I have not been wholly inactive. After the council at Springville, I went to Trezevant, where arrangements were made for a church school that I trust will be a blessing to the church and community. At Hoffasville a Sabbath School was organized. At Cross Plains a sister for whom many prayers have been offered took a decided stand for the truth, was baptized, and united with the church. . . . At Bowling Green we had good, and I trust profitable, meetings. Some are looking back to the world, but the zeal and hope of others are increasing. An earnest desire is expressed that a school be established here, where both races can be taught how to become 'laborers tighter with God.' May this hope be fully realized."

Kentucky Develops

"Perhaps you would like to know how the truth is progressing in Kentucky," wrote Bettie Coombs in a letter to the *Review* dated May 30, 1875. "May 15 and 16 Brother Osborn met with our little church at Locust Grove. The Lord blessed us in a great measure, and we had good meetings."

She then summed up the challenge facing Adventism at its starting point in Kentucky. "We are scattered, and our families are so divided that we find it a hard matter to meet. I often think the meetings are more highly appreciated, and the Lord is more precious to me than if we had no opposition and could meet every Sabbath.

"Last winter Brother Osborn labored some time in Green and Hart Counties, about 26 miles from here. Between 35 and 40 are keeping the commandments as the result of his labors. Some of them we think will make good, zealous workers in the cause of truth. Several were leading members in the Baptist church, and are of the best families in these counties.

"Our church, the 22nd and 23rd, met them at Powder Mills Chapel. Brother Osborn was free in the Lord, and I do not think I ever heard him speak with such liberty. His appointment was not fully circulated, as some of them live quite a distance from the church. Some were kept away by deaths and illness of their friends. He effected a temporary organization with 15 members, so that they could meet every Sabbath.

"We were much encouraged to see some of them take such an active part in the social meetings. Brother Osborn is receiving many calls to labor in other places. We believe much good can be done in this State. Could you not send a tent and some one to help? We feel anxious about many of our friends, as the truth is spreading so rapidly in other States. We believe if we could have tent meetings that many would come out and hear that would not otherwise."

Less than a year later, another correspondent came to the same conclusion. "From my home in Marshall, Michigan, I came to Kentucky about two months ago," wrote James K. Gilbert from Bowling Green in a letter dated January 24, 1876. "I have been employed with business most of the time, yet have circulated between two and three thousand pages of tracts, which are receiving a general perusal.

"At Lebanon Junction, I heard of some Sabbath keepers in Hardin County, whom I reached the ninth of this month. Here I learned of Brother Osborn's preaching in this section, and so returned 45 miles to meet with the brethren and listen to him.

"I found Brother Osborn in good spirits, and he was made welcome among the friends; but he had just arrived from Green County, where 24 had decided to obey the truth.

"I believe there are many honest hearts here, and they all call for more of the truth. I have found several who desire the *Review* and *Health Reformer*, and doubt not [that] a good work can be begun here at once.

"More laborers are needed in the harvest field. A tent is especially called for the coming season, and I have no doubt a glorious harvest may be secured as the result."

Limited Resources Blunt Impact

Having enough money to properly pay the ministers would be a problem in Kentucky for years to come. Conference President G.G. Rupert wrote in 1886, "Our ministers have lost a large portion of their valuable time by laboring in places that were not really favorable openings, simply because it was the best they could do without means. I hope our brethren will let this state of things exist in Kentucky no longer."

They did take advantage of opportunities in Metcalfe County: Squire Osborn in Edmonton and Orlando Soule in Glover's Creek, according to their 1877 *Review* dispatches. R.G. Garrett reported good and bad news out of Hart County that year. "Testimonies were free and tender, showing humility, a love for the cause of truth, and a determination to press forward in the good work," he wrote about the believers in Rio and Powder Mills. "But there are some who are not living up to the light they have; and they are losing their interest in the work."

Integrating the new converts into the church was difficult, because a church to make them part of simply did not exist.

Still, the gospel workers kept the new members busy. A tract and missionary society selling Adventist books and giving away literature was active by 1878. Membership was so small then that the president of the society, Clinton Owens, used the *Review* as a vehicle to announce quarterly meetings in the churches and urged all the scattered believers to attend one of them.

A Positive Spin on Struggles

In the August 15, 1878, *Review*, Secretary Bettie Coombs of Nolin, Kentucky, reported 45 members of the Kentucky and Tennessee Tract Society, and commented that they were off on a new venture.

"How thankful we should be that we have been enabled to accomplish as much as we have since the commencement of the year," she wrote. "This work was new to many of us when Bro. Haskell came South. Thanks to the Lord for his timely presence. I can see that our efforts in this direction have inspired some of us with more faith, hope and courage, and with a firmer trust in the Lord."

By the end of 1878, Clinton Owen could report much literature distribution and a few sales, with the state divided into two districts.

Reorganization

Members attending the 1879 camp meeting at Powder Mills, about 75 miles south of Louisville, decided to divide the states of Kentucky and Tennessee into separate conferences.

"The conference is greatly behind in the matter of transacting business properly, and in keeping its records," noted D.M. Canright, representing the General Conference. "Indeed, there was not a single set of blank books of any kind in the whole Conference. Steps were here taken to remedy this. The State secretary will attend the commercial college at Battle Creek. We find here more than an average proportion of really talented young women and several young men who can be very useful in the cause if they will but try. Quite a number will go immediately to our college."

Elder Canright also chaired the meeting organizing a state Sabbath School Association at Powder Mills at this same occasion and recommended "that each member pay one cent every week, that the treasury may not be empty."

During that year, R.G. Garrett related that he conducted meetings in Leitchfield, using the Morrison school house four miles out in the country. "The people manifest a great interest to hear, coming out in such numbers that the house will not hold half who come. There are some, however, who misrepresent and oppose us. None of the ministers have yet come to hear us."

According to the 1880 General Conference minutes, James and Ellen White hoped to work a bit in Kentucky but recommended that Elder J.O.

Corliss attend the camp meeting there should they be unable to go. They apparently did not, as things turned out.

More Evangelism

R.G. Garrett initiated meetings at Hanging Rock, resulting in 16 favorable responses and some bitter opposition, and reported several urgent requests to preach in Leitchfield. He was ordained to the gospel ministry at the 1880 camp meeting held at Rio.

Money a Constant Problem

Financial problems surfaced at the 1881 camp meeting held on a farm five miles east of Elizabethtown. The spirit was good, but the members were simply impoverished.

"Though poor in this world's goods, most of the brethren in the State seem disposed to lift what they can in the work; yet the Conference is in a somewhat crippled condition on account of lack of means to pay its preachers," wrote J.O. Corliss. "If this difficulty could be remedied, so that the ministers could be kept in the field constantly, I see no reason why their numbers might not increase rapidly. There is no finer country in the world than some parts of Kentucky, and the people certainly seem interested to hear the truth. It does seem a great pity to leave such a field without proper effort to sow the seeds of truth."

The Sabbath School Association elected Green Trent as president, R.G. Garrett as vice president, and Sallie Branstetter as secretary and treasurer at its fourth annual session in 1882.

The 1883 camp meeting gathered at Glasgow, "an old town, surrounded by good farming land, and situated about 80 miles south of Louisville and 10 miles east of the Louisville and Nashville Railroad. It has about 3,000 inhabitants, which are about equally divided between white and black. Its educational interests are among the finest in the State, two prominent colleges being located here."

The conference session reelected Squire Osborn as president and asked that Ellen White speak there sometime. "Could she do this, it would prove a great blessing to this young Conference," stated the report in the *Review*.

The Tract and Missionary Society placed as many books as it could in libraries that year. Bettie Coombs shared with *Review* readers letters of appreciation from librarians in Lexington, Bardstown and South Union, as well as Berea and Georgetown Colleges. She also related good responses received from canvassing in Glasgow, in preparation for camp meeting.

New Leadership

In 1884, G.G. Rupert moved to Kentucky to assist the overworked Squire Osborn, and reported to the *Review* office a $350 debt owed by the Tract and Missionary Society. "This would leave our society worth about $800, which would be very small considering the work that lies before us," he wrote. "In the coming year the tithe should at least be doubled; and we surely believe it will be if all will do their duty in the matter."

He also called for more canvassers. Help came from neighboring Ohio Conference in the form of a donation of 125 copies of *Thoughts on Daniel and Revelation,* to be sold for $1 each, and 500 subscriptions of the *Signs* for one year at 75 cents each, "the publications to be furnished on condition that there be legitimate subscriptions obtained for the same by the Kentucky Conference, either by individuals or in clubs, said publications to be furnished only as fast as such subscriptions are obtained." The conference estimated this missionary project would cost $15,000.

Outside Help

The Ohio Conference also gave a tent to their fellow believers. "We can assure them that while brethren Rupert and Saxby go to Kentucky assisted by our means as above indicated, they will have our prayers to follow them," stated the *Review* report of their state meeting.

S.N. Haskell praised Ohio for this unselfish act. "The President of the Kentucky Conference has labored alone for many years, and there is one feature of the work in that State which is gratifying," he wrote in the *Review*. "Notwithstanding the number of members is small, only 85 belonging to the Conference, those who have embraced the truth have done so by families; both parents and children are usually found serving God, and rejoicing in all points of present truth--spiritual gifts, the health reform, etc. The brethren in Ohio do not murmur at the loss of an acceptable laborer given to that southern field, which, with the removal of their President, has much reduced their ministerial force. There are now a sufficient number of laborers in Kentucky to run two tents, and although quite poor they raised means to purchase one. The Ohio Conference cheerfully gave them another. Then to encourage canvassers they voted to give them

500 copies of the *Signs* at half club rates, each, as fast as they obtained subscribers. The same offer was also made them on *Thoughts on Daniel and the Revelation* to the amount of $500. As these books will be sold and subscribers obtained at regular prices, this will give the Kentucky Conference $500 with which to carry on the work in that State. Said our Ohio friends, 'They have one of our men, now we will give them a tent, and some money to run it with, and they shall have our prayers.' This example is worthy to be followed by other Conferences that are better supplied with laborers than Ohio."

Still Possibilities

"After looking it all over, I believe Kentucky to be a good missionary field," Rupert wrote after visiting all the churches for the first time. "The numbers and financial strength are few and weak. But if all carry out the willingness to labor they claim to have, I can see no reason why they should not be equal, if not ahead, of any Conference among us, compared to numbers."

Rupert and R.M.J. Pound organized a Sabbath School in West Clifty in June, 1884, and held their own against serious opposition from local ministers. They also reported further success in Glasgow. Local ministers tried in vain to undo the work of W.H. Saxby and R.G. Garrett in the Nelson County town of Nelsonville. Rupert announced plans to start work in Burkesville and Hopkinsville.

"Last April Ohio made the Kentucky Tract Society the offer of fifty cents on every dollar's worth of *Signs* and *Thoughts* sold, to the amount of $500 and Whereas, this Conference stands in pressing need of said help; therefore Resolved, that we urge a thorough and continued canvass for *Thoughts on Daniel and the Revelation*, and especially for the *Signs*, as the above offer expires next April," reported the Tract and Missionary Society at its 1884 meeting.

Members at the 1884 camp meeting elected Elder Rupert president of the conference and ordained Willard Saxby to the ministry.

Financial Problems Still Hurt

"Our ministers who labored last season for a pittance are still unpaid," wrote G.G. Ruppert in the March 31, 1885, *Review*. "We know where the trouble lies. A hint to the wise is sufficient."

The quarterly meeting, held in May at the home of D.W. Barr in Elizabethtown, passed a resolution calling on "all of our members to pay their honest tithe" and to "avoid unscriptural marriages with unbelievers."

Evangelism Continues

G.G. Rupert and J.B. Forrest pitched a tent and conducted meetings in Madisonville starting on June 22, 1885, and a month later organized a church with 16 members. "Among the number were several between the ages of 35 And 50 that had never before made a religious profession," wrote Rupert.

W.H. Saxby won two converts at Nebo that summer. At Providence in Webster County, "a great tobacco center," 400 people attended his meeting at one point. He reported two baptisms, nine keeping the Sabbath, and 20 people attending Sabbath School.

The annual conference accepted the Madisonville Church and dropped the Seatonville and Summershade churches from the roster. The delegates also passed a resolution recommending that "our brethren, especially our young people, educate themselves with a view to laboring in the cause of God; and we recommend those of our young people who can possibly do so, to avail themselves of the benefits of our College at Battle Creek, Michigan."

Camp meeting later that year was held in Leitchfield, with the people pledging $500 towards a tent fund. I.D. Van Horn, a former treasurer of the General Conference and visitor to this camp meeting reported, "This meeting showed this Conference to be coming up in every branch of the work. Especially was this true in the canvassing department. A marked growth was seen also in the tithe and other finances. The meeting was small, but it stands among the best I have attended this season."

Upon returning to Madisonville towards the end of 1885, G.G. Rupert had good news for *Review* readers.

"I am happy to report that nearly every one that then started, is firm and growing," he wrote. "Pledges to our tent fund were taken to the amount of nearly $80. Every one voted to faithfully pay the tithe. Steps were taken to build a meeting house. An elder was ordained; three united with the church, and a tract society of 20 members was organized. Two able persons will engage in the canvassing work. We truly enjoyed our visit with them."

Rupert organized a church of 17 members in Leitchfield in 1886 and pitched a tent in Russellville. "Owing to rain and college commencement exercises, the attendance was not so large as we had expected," he wrote. "There are two colleges here: one conducted by the Baptists, the other by the Methodists. The town is old, and a great deal of pride and formality exist, which make it a hard field for reformation. We are favorably impressed with those who have taken hold of the truth, and are hopeful that they will prove to be true Christians."

He reported the Leitchfield Church off to a good start. "I see how faithfully some are keeping the tithe passbook; and it encourages me as nothing else can, to see those faithful for whom we labor," he wrote. A visit to Russellville showed him some of the interest there still remained.

R.G. Garrett closed meetings in Allensville with one person keeping the Sabbath. He found "a fair interest" in Daysville and went on to Adairville with "an average attendance of nearly 200 with a seemingly good interest to hear the truth."

Still Can't Lick the Financial Problem

Money apparently remained tight. The eleventh annual conference session, held at Bowling Green, passed a resolution saying "We are greatly crippled in our work because of a lack of means in this Conference; and it is evident that many of our people do not pay a full tithe; therefore, we resolve that we pledge ourselves to pay an honest tithe to the Lord hereafter."

The Conference also vowed to respond as soon as possible to a call for laborers from several Sabbath keepers in Louisville.

New Leadership

J.H. Cook, took over as conference president in 1887 and started out by visiting Elizabethtown, Leitchfield, Rio, and Knob Lick.

"Brethren Garrett and Pound were with me at Elizabethtown," he wrote in his first dispatch to the *Review*. "We held meetings with this church four days, which we believe were very profitable. Most of the brethren and sisters came from quite a distance, some on the cars, and others by private conveyance. The Lord came very near. At the close of our labors here, Brother Pound went to Mount Washington to hold a series of meetings, and he has since written me that he is having a good interest. In company with Brother Garrett, I next visited Leitchfield. Here they have a company of 15 Sabbath keepers, but some have so far departed from the faith that they did not attend the meeting; others manifested their interest by laying aside all worldly business, that they might be present. With one or two exceptions, all seemed anxious to know their duty. A tract society of nine members was organized."

Problems had crippled one of the pioneer churches in Hart County.

"We next visited the company at Rio [formerly known as Powder Mills]," Cook continued. "Here removals and apostasies have left but a small number. One was added by baptism. They seemed to gather fresh courage from this meeting, and as the plain truths of God's word were presented before them, it was evident that hearts were touched.

"From Rio we went to Knob Lick, 25 miles distant. The muddy condition of the roads presented traveling by wagon, but some came on horseback, and some of our brethren came from seven to 15 miles to attend this meeting. All seemed anxious to hear the word and understand their duty."

Elder Cook then appealed to the people to give enough money to enlarge their tent to make it 50 x 80 feet. He wrote that the people should pay as well as pledge enough money to meet this need.

A Low Point

The financial situation was desperate. "I wish to call the attention of brethren in Kentucky to the fact that our treasury is empty," he wrote in the March 1, 1887 *Review*. "Brethren Garrett, Pound and myself are trying to do what we can to spread the truth, but there are no means in the treasury to meet even our traveling expenses... I know that the good brethren in this State would not consent for a moment to have the ministers retire from the field. But what is to be done is a very grave question. We hope each one will stoop and inquire, Do I not hold some tithe in my hand that should be in the Lord's treasury?"

Powerhouse Minister Starts His Career

During this time, a future General Conference vice president spent an early portion of his ministry in Kentucky. The January 5, 1886, *Review* announced that Brother I.H. Evans of Michigan had joined the Kentucky Conference. He began by following up the work of Elders Rupert and Pegg in Leitchfield, reporting eight or ten people "rejoicing in the truth." Then he continued on to Rio. "They have a neat little church building, but many of the members have moved away, and the membership is small," he reported. He described the church at Glasgow as "so discouraged that but one or two families meet regularly for Sabbath meetings. A year ago last summer, Elder Rupert made a successful tent effort there, resulting in the organization of quite a church; but more than half have backslidden. Some, however, still belong to this church who are a great help to the cause in this State." Regarding Madisonville, "Elder Rupert organized a church here last summer, among whom I have found some warm-hearted friends. The brethren need to break off from some old habits, and come up on many points of our faith. They intend soon to build a house of worship."

Young Evans next conducted a tent effort in the Logan County town of Auburn before continuing on to Franklin.

In mid-1886, he reported on four communities. "We spent four weeks at Dalton, where seven embraced the truth, organized a Sabbath School since which they have united with the Madisonville Church." At Slaughterville, "We gave 10 discourses, creating quite an interest. Two embraced the Sabbath and other points of our faith." At Auburn, "we remained for six weeks, having only a fair audience. Ten took hold of the truth, and since have been trying to live it out." At Marion, "we remained four weeks. Fifteen adults began to keep the Sabbath, and we organized a Sabbath School of 30 members. We were obliged to leave a good interest, as the man on whose ground our tents were pitched desired us to move." At Princeton, "We have a good location. Have given two discourses to small audiences."

"Our courage is good," he concluded, "and we hope for brighter days for the cause in Kentucky."

I.H. Evans was ordained to the gospel ministry at the 1886 camp meeting held in Bowling Green and returned to Michigan in 1887. He became president of that conference four years later and went on to serve as treasurer and vice president of the General Conference, as well as president of the Asiatic Division, among other high offices.

Work in Small Places Continues

Some tithe money apparently came in, for the work continued robustly. Cook reported starting meetings to a good group in Glasgow. C.B. Hughes and R.G. Garrett pitched their tent near Randolph in Metcalfe County. Squire Osborn and R.M.J. Pound planned tent meetings in Shelby County, and Brother I.B. Palmer worked with them as a canvasser. Garrett and

Hughes later reported three new converts in Randolph but a disappointing reception in the Taylor County community of Campbellsville.

Prominent Adventist minister E.W. Farnsworth visited the 1887 camp meeting at Elizabethtown, "a thriving little village some 60 miles south of Louisville," and reported the pitching of ten family tents, five of which were put to use. "It is true, the cause in Kentucky has moved slowly," he wrote; "still it is advancing; and the meeting this year was in most respects the best we have ever attended here."

Some Response in Eastern Kentucky

From Bald Rock in Laurel County, J.H. Cook reported a good attendance and interest in meetings C.B. Hughes conducted there in the spring of 1888. "At one time it seemed as though the whole country would yield to the truth; but after time for reflection and when outside pressure commenced to fall heavily, the congregation began to decrease in number. From 21 who were keeping the Sabbath or promised to keep it, we now have 12 left. I have been with them for about two weeks, and Brother Hughes will stay with them one week longer, to strengthen those who remain. The people here are very poor, but they are very friendly, and are always willing to share what they have with you, and do it cheerfully. The work in Kentucky progresses slowly, but certainly God has a people here who will yet rally under the warning cry of the third message."

Soon after that, health problems of his wife forced Elder Cook to give up his work in Kentucky and move to the Pacific Coast.

Victory in Louisville

"The time from June 11 to 27, we spent in this city, aiding Brother Barry in an interest he had developed among some of the citizens of the place, under very interesting circumstances," G.G. Rupert wrote from Louisville in the July 10, 1888, *Review*. "About two years ago Brother Barry attended my tent meetings a short time in this State. He had read the *Signs* some before this, and he and his wife became deeply interested, and finally decided to obey. Being a Baptist minister, and employed especially in the temperance work as a lecturer, they observed the Sabbath in a quiet manner for some time, unbeknown to their friends. During the time, however, he used every means, but in the most cautious manner, to sow the seed among the best members of the church of which he was a member.

"The interest thus created finally developed, and before the minister in charge was aware of it, about a dozen of his church members had become Sabbatarians. These converts consisted of the organist, teachers in the Sunday school, and members of the choir, as well as the principal and some of the teachers of the public schools. The stir it made may be imagined. I reached the place at the hour when Brethren Barry and Hughes had a Bible reading appointed on the law and the covenants, which was to be attended by the editor of the Baptist paper. This proved a victory, and also the crisis. Charges were preferred against Brother Barry for teaching false doctrine, and his trial was set. At the time of this trial Brother Barry requested to make a defense to the charges. This request was refused, and he was promptly disfellowshipped. This course gave him many more friends. Then those who have embraced the Sabbath through his efforts arose and stated that they were in the same condition of faith and requested dismissal also. They were ruled out of order, and the meeting at once closed.

"These have now all covenanted together to keep God's commandments and to sustain Sabbath meetings. There is now a well-organized Sabbath School of over 30 members. I held meetings each evening with the brethren, and gave additional light on points of our faith. Others are interested and we believe a full course of lectures should be given soon. We feel to speak in praise to the quiet but wise course pursued by Brother Barry.

"We truly hope the time has come for a permanent prosperity in the work in Kentucky. There are many drawbacks here that we do not have in other fields. God has moved in his own providence in Louisville."

Another Setback

"There have been reverses and discouragements connected with the work in Kentucky for a few years past," wrote Dan T. Jones of the General Conference in the February 19, 1889 *Review*. "Last year they held no annual meeting, and the last General Conference thought best to put the work in Kentucky under the care of the Tennessee Conference, of which Elder William Covert was made president. After the matter had been talked over fully, the Kentucky brethren were reconciled to this new order of things. Still they expressed their determination financially to support their own work, and not become a burden to the Tennessee Conference, which already has as much in that direction as it can well carry."

Elder Covert was Tennessee-oriented but agreed to devote much of this time to overseeing the Lord's work in Kentucky. The following year, he reported having held meetings in Louisville, Leitchfield, Bowling Green, Russellville and Daysville, besides attending the state meeting at Rio.

"There are a few earnest ones at all these places who love the truth, and are trying to live it out," he wrote. "We regard Louisville as a favorable field of labor. It has a population estimated at 230,000. It is situated in a fertile district, with a healthful climate. It enjoys the shipping facilities of the Ohio River and eight lines of railroad. Coal and provisions are quite cheap. I have studied much about how the present truth is to be placed before the people of this city. The Kentucky tithe is not sufficient to pay laborers to go there, and do this work. The General Conference has its resources taxed to the uttermost in supplying labor and funds for other points. I can see but one line of operation within our reach. It is this: let a few good families of our people move to the city, who are able to make their own living, and at the same time, furnish a room for a Sabbath School and a station for canvassers, and engage heartily in the work of God."

A Strategy for the Larger Cities

He said the same applied to Nashville, Tennessee, a city with about half the population of Louisville. "We have several calls for meetings from persons who have embraced the Sabbath by reading, where meetings have never been held. We have only a few canvassers in the State, but there is room for many."

He urged all wishing to canvass to contact J.H. Dortch in Springville, Tennessee, and the believers to send their tithes to L.C. Heminger in Bowling Green.

Nothing Stops Evangelism

R.G. Garrett reported a good interest and attendance in the Ohio County town of Hamilton, with seven pledging to keep the Sabbath. The prospect of losing their jobs in the coal mines held some others back. "There is quite an undercurrent of opposition and prejudice on the part of many, and they did what they could to keep others from attending the meetings," he wrote.

R.M. Kilgore of the General Conference, working with C.M. Kinney, organized a black church in Louisville in 1890.

"We were pleased to note the willing mind with which the believers here accepted the plain testimony, and their actions with respect to it gave evidence that a work of grace was being wrought in their hearts," Kilgore wrote. "Ten adults represented themselves for church fellowship, and were accepted. Three were baptized by Brother Kinney. The name of this church is the 'First Louisville Church of S.D. Adventists.' Their tithe the last quarter amounted to about seventy-five dollars. A good beginning has been made; others are obeying the truth, and will soon unite with them."

R.G. Garrett began work in the Daviess County town of Owensboro on February 1, 1893, starting out by selling the book *Bible Readings*. "Many of the best people of the city are purchasers; ministers, merchants, Sunday school and church workers being of the number," he reported. "One lady has begun to observe the Sabbath, and others are much interested." He baptized an I.D. Moore and his wife and held some meetings in a Baptist house of worship.

Later that year he conducted meetings in a Methodist chapel in Southerland. The pastor later withdrew permission to use the chapel because "from what some of his brethren told him, our preaching was not suited to the spiritual growth of the church, and that some of the members were beginning seriously to question their authority for keeping Sunday instead of the Bible Sabbath, and were demanding scripture proof for the change."

He next conducted meetings to standing-room-only crowds in Utica. The local ministers did not like that.

"One of the ministers of this place preached against us, and another following; both of whom he reviewed before a large audience Tuesday night," wrote J.B. Thayer. "One of them, an old debater, had boasted great things, but both of them made so many contradictory and absurd statements against the commandments and the Sabbath that it was an easy matter to show their inconsistencies."

Garrett later wrote that he went back to Utica to find his crowd still there but locked out of a schoolhouse reserved for their meeting.

"Four have begun to keep the Sabbath, and others are almost persuaded to obey," he wrote. "Because of this, the dragon is wroth.

"The three ministers of the place and also one who came from Indiana for the purpose, have done what they could to oppose our work here, both by trying to keep the people away from our meetings and by public discourses," he continued. "We have several invitations to hold meetings in adjoining communities. We ask an interest in the prayers of all the brethren for the work here."

Some Sacrifice Comforts of Home

Thomas and Mary Ann Hughbanks wrote in the *Review* about leaving their Wisconsin home to do missionary work in Hopkinsville. "We would thank the friends of the cause of God for sending us reading matter, which we are distributing among the white and the colored people," they wrote. "The truth was new to the people here, many of them never having heard of Seventh-day Adventists or the third angel's message. We are giving reading matter to the members of three colored churches. They seem to be very anxious to read. Many of the older ones cannot read, and it will take patient labor to teach them the truth."

J.W. Collie moved to Louisville at the end of 1894 at the behest of the General Conference and found a small company "composed mostly of sisters, striving to hold up the light, and at the same time laboring under very discouraging circumstances."

Other workers soon joined him and his wife, and they conducted some meetings in the dead of winter, resulting in only a small attendance but some definite interest nonetheless. Meetings in the spring brought a better crowd.

Looking Up

Then in 1895, J.W. Collie wrote that about 30 people had accepted Adventism in Louisville. The canvassing work seemed to make impact, but the Adventists there lacked a suitable place to worship. The next year, Collie and M.W. Lewis conducted another series of meetings and expected another 35 decisions for Christ, even though the going was hard.

That summer, with favorable weather, Collie preached to congregations of from 150 to 400 people, despite being in a Catholic neighborhood, close to the convent walls. He reported 11 people taking their stand, including a lady with a responsible position in a leading brokerage firm.

He conducted another series of meetings in Louisville that summer of 1895, and reported a standing-room-only crowd. He had baptized six people from the previous series in the Ohio River and reported more calls for meetings than he could fulfill.

In 1896, Collie organized a church of 31 members and began looking for a house of worship. "The only available hall is on the third floor, and the first floor is occupied by a saloon," he wrote in the December 8, 1896, *Review*. "Finding that we could not secure the attendance of the people in this place, we have been occupying the double parlors of our home, which were fitted up as a chapel; but we have reached the limit of our capacity, and must look elsewhere. We desire very much a building of our own that will not only give our people a regular meeting-place, but will give character to our work in this city."

He reported a still-growing church, rising in spirit despite a turnover in workers in 1897.

I.R. Buster wrote in the June 29, 1897, *Review* that a fire almost destroyed a new tent that had just arrived in Louisville from Battle Creek.

A Miracle Saves the Day

""We took it to the home of one of our brethren for safe keeping till we could pitch it the following Tuesday," he related. "Monday night this brother's house caught fire, and was destroyed, with nearly all his household goods, and my books and bookcase; but God gave Brother Wingate's little 14-year-old girl, Hattie, strength to pull the tent and its belongs from the fire and smoke. This tent was so heavy that it required the united efforts of Brother Sheafe and myself to put it back in the place from which the child carried it. Not a rope or a pole connected with the tent was even scorched."

They pitched the tent and attracted an audience of about 100 black and white people. "So far as our tent meetings are concerned, the color line has 'gone a glimmering,' and the best class of people of all colors and shades with their families, touch elbows on the same seats and give the most diligent attention to the preaching of the word," he wrote. "All the boys and girls of the neighborhood are our staunch friends, and keep our tent and pulpit well supplied with beautiful flowers."

The next year, 1898, W.H. Saxby reported acquiring a "fine new hall" at 213 W. Walnut St. for Sabbath and Sunday evening services, a big improvement.

"Four workers from the Sanitarium spent most of the winter here," he reported. "Two schools of health were successfully conducted. Brother G.S. Vreeland had faithfully worked nearly 18 months in selling health publications in this city. Since the beginning of the present year, Brother E.W. Carey and Sisters Pierce and Wilson have been doing Bible work here. During the last three months an aged brother has sold $50 worth of the *Signs of the Times* from house to house, and over 300 copies of *His Glorious Appearing* and *Gospel Primer.*"

Church membership had climbed to 53.

"I have enjoyed much freedom in preaching, which has been largely of a practical nature, striving to build up the church in the different phases of the message," he wrote. "My courage was never better."

Penetrating Unentered Areas

Other Kentucky towns heard the Three Angels' Messages during these years. Missionary work began in Paducah and Mayfield in 1895 by C.G. and Nellie G. Lowry, parents of two future missionaries to Southern Asia. Mayfield was worked by J.D. Pegg and W.R. Burrow, who baptized three people. Other communities called for meetings.

J.N. Loughborough spent the month of February, 1898, visiting the Hazel and Bowling Green churches in Kentucky as well as Trezevant, Springville, Columbia, Nashville, Murfreesboro and Edgefield Junction in Tennessee. Effectively challenging with tracts from the Religious Liberty Association a Sunday reform movement, Lewis C. Sheafe revived the Lexington Church. C.P. Bollman continued the tent evangelism in Paducah.

R.G. Garrett baptized two people in Randolph and saw a Baptist minister and his son accept Adventism in Utica. He also reported baptizing three people at Render and two people at Higdon. Calls went out for meetings in Hickory Grove, Sedalia and Boydsville.

W. R. Burrow and C. G. Lowry responded, finding people receptive to their preaching in all these places.

A Lasting Impact

In the January 4, 1898 *Review*, new convert Walter Jones wrote of organizing a Sabbath School in Sand Hill. It later fell apart, but he persisted in visiting those who kept their newfound faith.

Then, when he was expecting to conduct a Sunday-morning meeting in a tent, somebody came on Saturday night and cut all but one of the ropes.

"It was done so quietly that I did not hear them, though only a short distance from the tent," Jones wrote. "Still, the Lord overruled. At half past two, I look[ed] out, and as the moon was shining brightly, saw the tent down. Finding that they had only cut the ropes, I notified the brethren living from one to two miles away, and before time to open the meeting, we had the tent up better than before. The Lord's hand was seen during our whole stay of three weeks, counteracting the purpose of opposing powers. Two precious souls are now walking in the light as the result of the work there, and seed has been sown that will, I believe, bring forth for the reaping time. The Lord enabled me to maintain a sweet spirit amid it all. Six have united with the church since I first went there, three years ago, and these last two will unite. There are others who I think will do so when the opportunity is presented. A Sabbath school of about 25 members is enrolled there. The work is encouraging, though at one time it looked as if the efforts made to advance the truth were in vain. May the Lord continue to bless the work."

The Powder Mills Seventh-day Adventist Church held many early important Adventist meetings, one of which decided to divide Kentucky and Tennessee into separate conferences in 1879.

Results

Many of these churches are still alive and bearing fruit. While Kentucky never became a center for Adventist institutional activity, its churches have contributed many outstanding people to the denominational work.

East Tennessee Develops

For many years after the Civil War, most Adventist activity occurred in the middle and western parts of Kentucky and Tennessee. The mountainous eastern regions were harder to develop. Though the Tennessee River originated in the east, shoals in northern Alabama prevented unobstructed navigation to the Ohio and then Mississippi Rivers until the coming of the Tennessee Valley Authority (TVA) in the 1930s.

The General Conference therefore regarded the eastern halves of Kentucky and Tennessee as mission fields, with the Tennessee River Conference comprising the western parts of Kentucky and Tennessee. East Tennessee was referred to as the Cumberland Mission in the *Review* dispatches.

Nevertheless, the Adventist influence found its way to East Tennesseans. Earnest seekers for truth there also wrote for help to grow in their newfound faith and had their share of opposition and threats.

Early Carolina Connections

An L.P. Hodges mentioned in the July 26, 1881, *Review* that he and a Brother Kime intended to cross the North Carolina state line and visit bordering Unicoi and Carter Counties.

"The interest is good in Eastern Tennessee," he wrote. "We need laborers here." "Brother Kime and myself visited East Tennessee, as stated in my last report," he commented a few weeks later. "We traveled on foot through the hot sun, the rain, and the mud, upwards of 150 miles. The people were kind to us during our stay with them. They heard us willingly, and want us to come back. We hope to return in the fall, and follow up the interest that has been awakened. East Tennessee is a good field of labor."

Hodges was based in Watauga County, N.C., but the calls from across the state line kept him going back.

"I have received several letters from East Tennessee within a few days; three of these were from Unicoi County, one from Blount County, and one from Green County," he wrote in the November 8, 1881, *Review*. "The writers all say they believe Saturday is the true Sabbath, and request us to come back there and preach to them. These men write that all the old citizens in that country are reading their Bibles with great eagerness, to see if these things are so. This is the result of a visit by Brother Kime and myself to that section the first of August last. It seems that the doctrines of Seventh-day Adventists are making quite a stir in East Tennessee. I think some good can be done there with the proper labor."

Hodges apparently worked hard and well in this Appalachian mission field, because by the middle of 1886, he hoped to organize a conference in Western North Carolina and East Tennessee.

More People Respond in Other Areas

By 1890, dispatches from East Tennessee were published in the *Review* under the heading of Cumberland Mission Field.

J.W. Scoles reported four people keeping the Sabbath in Dayton as the result of meetings Elder J.M. Rees had held there two years before, and another 20 had signed the Sabbath covenant at the conclusion of his own meetings.

"A Sabbath School of 40 scholars has been organized, and supplied with necessary helps, and we hope to effect a church organization soon," he wrote.

More Opposition

Along with the Scoles report, the *Review* ran a notice from the Dayton local newspaper showing that he may have been fearfully effective.

"A few weeks ago a Seventh-day Adventist minister from California by the name of J.W. Scoles was sent to East Tennessee by his church to do missionary work in behalf of that organization," began an article in the March 21, 1890, Dayton *Leader*. "He located in Graysville, and a short time afterward began a series of meetings in this city, and, it is said, made a number of converts to his creed. He is said to be an earnest and intelligent speaker, and discoursed upon abstruse scriptural doctrines peculiar to his church, but advocated the same standard of ethics that is accepted and preached by all theologians and moralists of whatever creed. From what we have been able to learn, he has transgressed no moral law, but has simply expounded his scriptural doctrines and advocated his creed, as all other preachers do every day in the year. Notwithstanding our boasted liberality, blind bigotry has asserted itself in this instance, as the following note, which Mr. Scoles received through the Dayton post office last Monday morning, will show, and which we give verbatim.

"'Mr. Scoles we Notify you in Short to leave this town and Never More Return know We Will give You till Monday Morning to leave In, and if you Do not leave you May take What follows. We W O'

"This is an infamous outrage," continued the opinion piece. "Our Constitution and advanced civilization guarantee to every man the right to worship God according to the dictates of his own conscience, and every one who would deny a man this right is an enemy to free government and free thought. We neither indorse nor condemn Mr. Scoles's doctrines; for we do not know anything about them. If he is satisfied with them, and conforms to a pure standard of morals, every one else ought to be.

"We do not think he will submit to bulldozing and will likely be in town next Monday."

Threats Fail to Intimidate

R.M. Kilgore, who headed this region of the South for the General Conference, visited the Cumberland Mission Field in midsummer and found Elder Scoles and his wife preparing to start another series of meetings. "I spoke on Monday night at Dayton on Religious Liberty," he wrote. "The late decision of the Supreme Court of Tennessee, in the case of Brother King is awaking public sentiment both pro and con on this subject. Those who clamor for legal enactments to prop up and sustain the tottering papal Sunday, become more defiant and intolerant as such judgments are rendered, while the oppressed are driven to their knees, and seek more earnestly the face and favor of Him who rules in heaven."

Inroads in Other Places

W.C. Dalbey reported the conclusion of a four-week series of meetings in Brayton the next year and having sold about 1,000 pages of Adventist reading matter. He went on to Dunlap and conducted meetings there with A.P. Heacock, preaching to between 50 to 150 people.

Grant Adkins also reported working at Dunlap with Brother Heacock and went on to Kiouki, "a small settlement on Walden's Ridge, where we had an invitation to hold some meetings." He found little interest there but reported that a company at the Cove had a 23-member Sabbath School. "May God help this dear little company to stand firm under the present outburst of persecution which some are wont to urge upon them," he wrote. "Some are lying in ambush, like a coyote, to catch them working on Sunday, so as to report them to the grand jury."

Brother Dalbey continued working in Dunlap and by mid-1891 reported not much to show in the form of converts perhaps, but a solid interest in spite of serious opposition. He next went to Delphi.

"We hope that there may yet be more effective work done in this place," he wrote. "Some have acknowledged the truth, but the people seem slow to act and cautious, not only because we are from the North, but because they have not full confidence in us as a denomination. Realizing this fact, we feel like continuing the labor here, asking the prayers of God's people that his truth may at last triumph in this place, and that there may yet be a company raised up that will hold up the standard of truth here."

Heacock left a few keeping the Sabbath in Dunlap and went on to South Pittsburgh. "This is a town of from three to four thousand inhabitants, having street cars and being lighted with electricity, and is a veritable Pittsburgh for furnaces and foundries," he wrote. "Our work in this valley is entirely new. Many where we have labored believe the truth and desire to obey."

The next year he reported from Antioch and Brayton, noting mainly an encouraging response with perhaps possibilities for the future.

"Our work in this valley is entirely new," wrote A.P. Heacock in the January 12, 1892 *Review*, writing from Dunlap, Pittsburgh and Kimball. "Many where we have labored believe the truth and desire to obey; but they dread to take hold in the face of our stringent Sunday law, with so few to sustain each other as there are here. If some of our good families of Sabbath keepers in the North would only decide to come here and live out the truth, they would find it a pleasant place to live, and at the same time be doing effectual missionary work."

Grant Adkins sounded optimistic about the Graysville Church early in 1892, especially with the presence of a school committee and powerful sermons by the conference leadership.

"Since my last report, we have held meetings about seven weeks, in a hall at South Pittsburgh," wrote A.P. Heacock in the May 31, 1892 *Review*. "Two signed the covenant here. Many are convinced of the truth, and some of these desire to obey, but have not the faith to step out, as they will at once be thrown out of employment, with no prospect of anything to do by which to earn a living."

He added that one man wanted to sell his property and move to a more favorable location, and that a Methodist minister had bought *Thoughts on*

Daniel and the Revelation by Uriah Smith. Of the various approaches tried, health and temperance worked seemed to generate the most favorable response in the South.

Some of his new converts at Dunlap and Delphi were keeping the faith. The interest in South Pittsburg was still strong later in the year.

The big boss, R.M. Kilgore, reported a commendable general meeting in Asheville, N.C., in mid-1893 and also fine prospects in Morristown and Knoxville.

Effective Evangelism Among the Blacks

Then, writing from Knoxville, J.E. and Julia F. Caldwell saw possibilities in working for black people there.

"We were greatly surprised and gratified to find as much ability and culture among the colored population as we did," they commented in the July 25, 1893, *Review*. "They are higher than we had been led to think. The masses seem wholly given up to pleasure-seeking, but here and there among them are those who sigh and cry on account of the abominations done in their midst. These are hungry for a better knowledge of God. They appear to realize the fallen condition of the churches and of society in general. We have not yet seen many of them brought to the testing points of the message for today, but a few have counted the cost, and declare themselves ready to follow the light of the word."

They related some inspiring stories of people responding to the message but saw a need for a school for the training of black young people.

"Already some of our young people are talking of entering the field as workers," they wrote. "Brethren, tell us what we can say to them. They must receive training before they can be encouraged to do much; but where can we send them? Will not some one whom the Lord has entrusted with means, use it to establish and maintain a school for colored people in the South? The school at Graysville for whites is appreciated and trusted of men and blessed of God. But the colored work will be crippled and hindered until they, also, have a school."

The Message Spreads Still More

In July, 1893, Grant Adkins reported a strong company in Fountain City. "All are not free from trials and temptations, however," he wrote. "The enemy rather prefers Tennessee as a field of labor."

"Some months ago I reported work done in Morgan County, since which time I have engaged in labor as the way opened in this and adjoining counties," wrote J.W. Scoles in mid-1893. "A church of 11 members has been organized near Webster, Roane County, and two very intelligent ladies have recently begun the observance of the Sabbath near Pin Hook Landing, Meigs County. Others in this vicinity are investigating, and calls are coming in for a full course of meetings. Two weeks ago I received two more members into the church at Webster, and administered baptism to one. Thus the work is going, and God's people are being given the special truths which are to sanctify them for his work here, and fit them up to dwell in his presence eternally hereafter."

The work of Dr. J.E. Caldwell in Knoxville and Fountain City impressed Charles E. Sturdevant when he followed it up in 1894. "The work done by Dr. Caldwell was done with the right motive, and those who received the truth from him show what manner of entering in he had unto them," he observed. "They miss him very much, and it would be a great help if a good medical missionary could labor in this city. . . Our chief anxiety is that the high tone of the work pitched here by Brother Caldwell and his co-laborers may not be lowered now; for we have no time for any backward steps."

Writing from Spring City in mid-1895, R.M. Kilgore reported "tokens of a gain in interest and in numbers attending the meetings." A Methodist minister invited him to address his congregation on tithes, played the organ and led the singing for his meetings, and ordered a full set of charts on Daniel and Revelation. Some of the city officials also attended despite receiving a letter advising them to stay away. Somebody in Graysville had sent a card into town saying "The Advents are making for your town with a tent, for a meeting; now is the time to nip them in the bud, and not be bothered with them." Kilgore had heard of an anti-Adventist book being sent there but thought it would help him sell more Ellen White literature. "Brother England being called home by sickness in his family, I am alone with my wife, yet I am not alone," he wrote. "I am of good courage in the Lord, for he is with me."

E.L. Sanford reported new converts in Harriman after he had conducted Sabbath and Sunday meetings there. "If some brethren who are farmers could come here to show the people how to farm and at the same time live the truth out before them, it would be a great blessing," he wrote.

R.M. Kilgore reported a membership of 55 people, mostly black, in the Knoxville Church early in 1896. "They make a strong appeal for labor to be bestowed upon the white population of the city, and it ought to be done," he wrote. "There is also a crying need for a house of worship."

Kilgore went back to Spring City and found his new converts there still keeping the faith. Five people accepted the Sabbath in Evensville, and the Graysville Church was still strong despite losing two members. "Since the close of the Graysville school in April, 16 of the students and teachers have gone to work in several departments of the cause, and encouraging reports are received that success attends their efforts," he wrote. Things were also going well for him in Rockwood.

Charles E. Sturdevant and his wife reported a lively interest in Uoeba, with some having freed themselves from tobacco, swine's flesh, and snuff.

Grant Adkins had beneficial visits with the believers in Cove, Graysville and Harriman, and then settled in to work for a few weeks in Knoxville before the 1896 camp meeting.

R.M. Kilgore continued his work in Tennessee during 1896 by conducting meetings in Rockwood, reporting a thirst for truth but a serious crisis looming before those committing to keeping the Sabbath.

Sabbath Work and Over-Extension Problems

"The most discouraging feature which confronts us here is the fact that nearly all our hearers are in the employ of the Roane Iron Co., whose furnaces yield an output of about 150 tons of pig iron daily," he wrote. "It is estimated that five men are required to produce a ton of iron. Whether many or few will obey God and suffer discharge from the employment which yields them a living, is yet to be determined."

Another problem was that "Calls are coming in for us to go to other places when we close up here," meaning the best he could do was hope the people would seriously study the books he sold them. Following through with organization was difficult when he was spread too thin and had too much territory to cover.

A serious crisis must have gripped Graysville that year, because W. Woodford wrote in the June 16, 1896, *Review* of a day of fasting and prayer there, stating, "The battle is raging; soon all will be over, the victory complete." The next month, Woodford announced starting meetings in Chattanooga, with only 18 people attending opening night. "The attendance has grown, however, and the past few nights over 100 have attended; the interest to hear is on the increase," he wrote.

The *Review* carried a special notice of the Graysville Academy opening in the fall of 1896, along with Walla Walla College. "The general management and plan of work is now similar to that of our older colleges and academies in the North," read the announcement. "Four courses of study, namely, scientific, classical, Biblical and commercial are offered." W.T. Bland signed the announcement.

R.M. Kilgore next carried the banner of truth into Cleveland, attracting a crowd of between 65 on opening night to 400 later on. Negative reports from the Rhea County trials seemed to have made it difficult but not impossible for him there.

Mr. and Mrs. Charles E. Sturdevant reported a Sabbath School of six, including two children, in Nast. They evangelized Harriman, Sugar Grove and Daisy Dell as well. The Sturdevants made their home in Harriman and also worked at Webster, but Harriman seemed to be where they found the best response. They reported a Professor R.B. Taggart and his wife keeping the Sabbath there. They also visited Knoxville and Webster and followed up the work of J.W. Scoles and Grant Adkins in Daisy Dell.

Promoting the School

W.T. Bland kept Graysville Academy before the people, advertising the school for another year in the summer of 1897. "This school, located in Southeastern Tennessee, near Chattanooga, is in the center of the great Southern district, where there are more than 15 million people to whom the third angel's message must now be carried," he wrote. "The courses of study and general plans of the school are arranged with special reference to the work in the South, which is now the greatest missionary field in the country."

J.N. Loughborough attended a district conference in Graysville late in 1897 and reported preaching in a substantial meeting house seating over 200 people.

"It seems to me that Graysville valley is an excellent place for a school of this character," he wrote. "At this time the hills surrounding the valley, and their various tints of autumn leaves, interspersed with evergreen pines, presented a view of nature which it was a delight to see. The Lord came very near to us in the Conference. He has spoken to us in plain terms of what should be done in the South, and it was very evident that angels of God were hovering near as we sought the Lord for his Spirit and guidance in the work."

Progress Continues

Late in 1898, E.H. Gates found two Sabbath-keeping families in Harriman: Brother and Sister Sturdevant and Professor Taggart and his wife. "We have organized a Sabbath School of about 14 members, and a few weeks ago organized a branch school a mile from town among the poor children," he wrote.

Grant Adkins joined Brother Gates in conducting a 10-day meeting in Briceville and then visited isolated believers in Knox County. They also visited some new converts of Brother Sturdevant in Shooks, and then conducted a regional meeting consisting of people from Aswan, Fountain City, and Beorden, as well as Shooks.

In reporting for the Cumberland Mission Field, E.H. Gates wrote he operated out of Harriman but also gave reports for Louisville, Newport, Georgetown and Rowland, Kentucky. He reported organizing a church of 22 members in Harriman and an active church in Chattanooga.

"Calls are coming in for labor in different places," he wrote.

Persecution Won't Go Away

The final dispatch from East Tennessee for the 19th century came out in the May 30, 1899, *Review* in the form of a court challenge to George M. Powell, who had left Michigan with his wife to start a school near Sanford.

"January 19, but three days after the opening of our school, a deputy sheriff arrested four of us—Brother and Sister Bristol, my wife, and myself—for working on Sunday," he wrote in the May 30, 1899 *Review*. "We each gave bonds for $250, being permitted to become surety for one another. Brother Bristol's crime was that of hauling cornstalks on Sunday, and myself and wife were charged with washing on Sunday 'to the common nuisance.'

"The regular spring term of circuit court convened at Athens, April 10, and we were all on hand to be 'judged' as we supposed, 'for the hope of the promise made of God unto our fathers.'

These families decided to go through this ordeal on their own.

"Brother Bristol's case came up the first day of the session, and the evidence developed the fact that he was in the habit of hauling a small load of stalks daily, the same being a part of his chores," Powell continued. "The jury retired, and in a few minutes returned a verdict of 'not guilty.' Sister Bristol's case was thrown out of court. This was about what we expected in these cases.

"My case was taken up the second day, and only one witness appeared against me,--the man who had us indicted. He swore that the washing, which we had done quietly and in a secluded spot, was a nuisance, disturbing the neighborhood, and causing much talk. Upon being further questioned, his own testimony proved that he was the only man who saw it, and that the neighbors knew nothing of the affair till it was blazed abroad by himself, and the only disturbance was caused by himself. The case went to the jury without argument;' and in less time than it takes to write it, a verdict of 'not guilty' was returned.

"All the officials of the court treated us fairly and kindly throughout, and the good Spirit prevailed in the court room."

The Charges Enlarged Their Audience

"One of the most influential men in this vicinity, a prosperous farmer, was so interested in our welfare that he, unsolicited of course, made a special trip to Athens, to inform all whom he could that we were good citizens, and ought not to be prosecuted," Powell added.

So the development of Adventism followed the same pattern all across the state: acceptance, opposition and triumph--big time in East Tennessee. The Cumberland Mission became the Cumberland Conference in 1900 and merged into the Georgia-Cumberland Conference in 1932. Its churches grew and contributed many outstanding people to the denomination. Graysville Academy developed into Southern Training School and moved out of town to a more rural location near Chattanooga in 1916 and became Southern Adventist University in Collegedale, Tennessee, now one of the flagship colleges of the Seventh-day Adventist Church.

Epilogue

And so the 19th century Adventist endeavors in Kentucky and Tennessee ended as they began, with threats staring them in the face all the way.

Persecutions, like revivals, sooner or later die down and slip into the background. But a substantial church operating good schools can, ironically, be less of a challenge to the outside world than a small, struggling religious group if the members try to head off persecution through compromise.

For persecution to become a thing of the past and largely forgotten as the church attains respectability is to run the risk of going off message. Churches, schools and hospitals will come and go. Times will change. But not how good or bad times would get, a remnant will always be faithful and must remember that keeping the church a threat to the forces of evil requires sacrifice and loss of popularity.

TEACH Services, Inc.
PUBLISHING

We invite you to view the complete
selection of titles we publish at:
www.TEACHServices.com

We encourage you to write us
with your thoughts about this,
or any other book we publish at:
info@TEACHServices.com

TEACH Services' titles may be purchased in
bulk quantities for educational, fund-raising,
business, or promotional use.
bulksales@TEACHServices.com

Finally, if you are interested in seeing
your own book in print, please contact us at:
publishing@TEACHServices.com

We are happy to review your manuscript at no charge.